# Creating the Future Together

# Creating the Future Together

## Methods to Inspire Your
## Whole Faith Community

Loren B. Mead and Billie T. Alban

THE
ALBAN
INSTITUTE

Herndon, Virginia
www.alban.org

The Alban Institute
2121 Cooperative Way, Suite 100
Herndon, VA 20171-5370

Unless otherwise noted, all Scripture quotations are from the New Revised Standard Version of the Bible, copyright © 1989, Division of Christian Education of the National Council of the Churches of Christ in the United States of America, and are used by permission.

Scripture quotations marked NIV are from the Holy Bible, New International Version, copyright © 1973, 1978, 1984 by International Bible Society. Used by permission of Zondervan Publishing House. All rights reserved.

Scripture quotations marked KJV are from the King James Version of the Bible.

Cover design by Tobias Becker, Bird Box Design.

Library of Congress Cataloging-in-Publication Data

Mead, Loren B.
  Creating the future together : methods to inspire your whole faith community / Loren B. Mead and Billie T. Alban.
    p. cm.
  ISBN 978-1-56699-364-7
  1. Church group work.  I. Alban, Billie, T., 1925- II. Title.

BV652.2.M43 2008
253'.7—dc22

2008013329

12  11  10  09  08      VG      1  2  3  4  5

This book is dedicated to Carl Dudley.

*In appreciation for his pioneer witness
to the power of congregations in communities.*

# Contents

# Foreword

WHICH IS MORE DIFFICULT TO CHANGE, A RELIGIOUS ORGANIZATION, the focus of this book, or an academic institution, where I spend most of my time? It is probably a toss-up as to which type of organization occupies first place for most resistant to change. Assuming that my premise for strength of resistance is reasonably accurate, why might this be so?

Not the only reason, but a fundamental one, is that both religious organizations and academic institutions are bastions of society. Their missions and *raisons d'etre* are to uphold critically important values for civilization—beliefs, attitudes, and values that transcend individual self interests, on the one hand, and the production of knowledge and education, on the other. Leaders and members of these two kinds of organizations believe that they have a moral obligation to uphold standards that undergird a civilized society, that promote goodwill among people, and that enlighten and enhance general well being.

And there are rights and ceremonies that reinforce these standards in both the religious and academic worlds, such as baptisms, bar mitzvahs, and celebrations, or tenure, titles for faculty, and conferring of degrees. To consider changing any aspect of these standards, rites, and deeply held beliefs about what is right is close to blasphemy.

Civilizations rise and fall, trends come and go, societal conflicts continue to disrupt, so there must be some things that remain stable and reliable and do not change to ensure that civil behavior, beliefs in a higher force than oneself, and increased enlightenment are upheld.

Yet changes in the larger environment for these organizations occur and ever more rapidly. In fact, recent evidence shows that now the external environment changes more rapidly than organizations seem to be able to change themselves if they are to respond effectively. At the same time the external environment is more complex than ever before. Survival for these organizations is dependent on clarity about what needs to change and what needs to remain and perhaps be strengthened. As Mead and Alban emphasize, this clarity must begin with the organization's external environment. Following an analysis of the external environment, with particular focus on those forces that have the most direct impact on the organization (demographic shifts, obtaining capital for financing the organization, generational differences, etc.), attention is then concentrated on the organization itself, with initial emphasis on mission, strategy, leadership and organizational culture.

While religious organizations and academic institutions remain bastions of society, even they are confronted with needs for change. Whether to change is not the question. It is a matter of what and how much to change—some or sweeping?

It has become much clearer today that if significant or sweeping change is required to ensure long-term effectiveness, or even basic survival, methods of continuous improvement (improving quality of service or reducing bureaucracy), will not lead to change that fundamentally affects the organization. We consider organizational change today in two broad categories: as either continuous or discontinuous and episodic, for example, or as transactional or transformational, for another, or as evolutionary or revolutionary, for yet another. And it is the latter terms—episodic, transformational, and revolutionary—that convey what is required for fundamental change. For deep-seated change to occur, a "jolt" to the system is required. In the organizational change literature this jolt is referred to as a *perturbation*, ironically a term that comes from evolutionary theory.

Often the hue and cry of people in positions of organizational leadership is something like, "We need to change our ways of doing things"—that is, our culture—or "We need to change people's mindsets." The need for change is identified, but how to do it is not. This is understandable. Changing culture and mindsets is not exactly a walk in the park. After all, culture resides largely in the background, not in the foreground, of our daily behavior and is more below the surface of consciousness than readily obvious. The norms we conform to (more often than not without conscious thought) and the values we uphold constitute collectively the organization's culture. Identifying these patterns, much less changing them, takes time, diligence, focus, and energy on the part of organizational leaders and members.

In the beginning stages of originating and building any organization, choices are made that then become deep-seated if not practically immutable. At the outset decisions are made about, say, the desire to locate authority less centrally, to interact with one another informally on a first-name basis rather than formally, to follow a creed or mission that represents what members of the organization strongly believe and want to stand for, to insure that matters of finance and budgeting are transparent rather than secretive, to respect and follow people in positions of leadership rather than undermine their actions, etc. These choices that early on are made gradually become taken for granted, followed without much thought, never questioned, and years later organizational members are not likely to be able to explain why they do certain things the way they do them. "It's just the way we do things here."

"These ways of doing things here" constitutes the culture and this ingrained behavioral process is difficult to even identify, much less change. But there are times when change is a necessity for long-term survival. Should the need for change be cultural in nature, not, for example, merely a slight shift in direction, then a jolt to the system is needed.

A jolt to the system can take several different forms. In an organization where the top executives saw no need for large-scale change but the CEO and an external consultant did, the decision was made to pull aside the number two executive for a month to prepare a special presentation for the top 100 executives. The presentation was based on an intensive study of the organization's external environment, particularly its marketplace. With elaborate data presented using many charts, the executive showed clearly and dramatically that if the company continued with business as usual they would be out of business in five years. This presentation made by an executive with considerable credibility served as the jolt necessary for serious change to be undertaken.

Another example of a jolt is when two organizations merge, or when a large acquisition is made where the acquired organization is almost as large as or even larger than the acquirer. This kind of action usually requires a change in culture.

Another possibility of a jolt is the subject of this book. A large-scale intervention—getting most if not the entire system in the same room at the same time—can serve as a jolt to the system. "We've never done such a thing before."

We know that for significant and fundamental change in an organization to occur, revolutionary and transformational actions must be taken. We also now know the importance of leadership and the involvement of organizational members in the change process. Commitment to the change on the part of many, hopefully all, members and constituents of the organization is key. Enter Mead and Alban. This book of theirs for faith communities is a highly valuable contribution. Their contribution is the provision of concepts, ideas, and methods that are tried and true regarding what we know that works for lasting change in organizations.

W. Warner Burke
Edward Lee Thorndike Professor of
Psychology and Education
Teachers College, Columbia University

# Acknowledgments

First, WE WOULD LIKE TO THANK OUR EDITOR, BETH GAEDE. WE greatly benefited from her skillful editing, her unique ability to bring clarity to our writing, and her continuous encouragement.

We also want to acknowledge all those who contributed stories to this book:

Brian Roberts
Steve Croft
Jean Haskell
Julie Liedman
Doug Germann
Neil Newman
David Taylor
Sandra Janoff
Anna Aramini
Vance Johnson
Mary Sharer Johnson
Edward Hall
Melanie Guste
Jean Bartunek
Lisa Beutler
Richard Pearson

Finally, we thank our families, friends, and the Rev. Jerry Zimmerman, who put up with us, encouraged us, and gave helpful feedback.

# Chapter 1
# Engaging Change

"CHANGE" IS ONE OF THE MOST TROUBLESOME WORDS IN religious circles today. Everyone struggles with it. The world around us changes, we change, and the people we work with and serve change. Yet we are afraid of change—the resistance and the anger it may release and the demands it may make on us. We read daily in newspapers about the divisiveness that issues of change have caused in many religious organizations. We often ignore the issues and hope they will go away. Nonetheless, this book is about change in those very circles—especially in congregations, regional structures of denominations, religious communities, and institutions of theological education.

In this fast-changing world it has become increasingly clear that organizations that don't find ways to adapt to the changes around them don't survive. A sign of health in an organization—indeed, even in a system like the human body—is the ability to respond to the environment it lives in. The healthy body has a capacity to sense what's going on around it and to make adaptations or fight what's going on in its changing world. Churches, seminaries, universities, denominational offices, and businesses all have to realize that the world around them is changing and that they have to adapt their life and operations to change. This book is about approaches that have helped both congregations and religious organizations to engage change. There is no magic formula, but several methods

1

have proved helpful to other religious communities, and we offer them here.

Two of us are writing this book together. Billie Alban, a lifelong member and participant in congregations, has spent her professional life as a teacher, consultant, and writer. Her specialty is in organization dynamics. Loren Mead has spent most of his professional life as an Episcopal clergyman, focusing on the life and work of religious institutions. He has become known for his consulting, teaching, and writing in those fields. Both of us love the religious organizations that have given us life. Both of us have been frustrated by the difficulty religious organizations face in making choices that involve necessary changes.

## A Review of Your Situation

In this first chapter, we share with you two checklists that may help you think about your own work in your current setting. The first list is for religious congregations. The second list is for other institutions, such as judicatory bodies, theological seminaries, ecumenical organizations, and the like. If your primary focus is congregations, we encourage you to work through the institutional list as well. Likewise, if you work with an institution, go back and try out the questions in the congregational checklist. Either list may trigger further thoughts about change.

You may decide after completing the checklist assessment that none of the issues listed resonates with you. We want to encourage you, however, to explore further. You might give the checklist to members of your board or another appropriate group. Issues around change often trigger very different feelings and perceptions among members of an organization. You may be surprised to find that some members of your board agree with you but have been hesitant to speak up. Others may perceive reality very differently and have perspectives and insights different from your own. If that is true, the checklists may, at the very least, lead to an interesting discussion. If you do identify important concerns—either agreement about important issues or sharp differences of opinion—you may want to consider using one or more of the methods in this book to *engage the whole system* in creating a preferred future. That's a place to start.

We do *not* suggest that you give everyone in a congregation or other organization the checklists. If you and your leaders agree there are important issues to discuss, we recommend that you use one of the large-group methods described in chapter 3. These methods allow people to talk to each other in constructive ways as the community sits down and "reasons together." You will find out what is on the minds and hearts of the members and stakeholders as they think about the future of the organization in a changing world.

We are writing this book in the hope that it will help your community wrestle with the challenges facing organizations today. Many of the issues on the checklist cannot be solved by individuals or by members of special committees. These issues are bigger than any of us. Organizations need, as we call it here, "the system in the room." Your "system," however you define it, includes people who care about the items on the checklist. It includes stakeholders, both internal and external, whose wisdom and experience are needed to generate and support change. You want them on board, because you need their help. "You Don't Have to Do It Alone" is one of the primary themes of this book.

Since the early 1990s sustained efforts have been made to develop methods for addressing just such complex issues. A whole new field of organizational dynamics has been growing, dedicated to helping complex organizations like yours face just such complicated issues. In this book we want to introduce you to some of the methods that have been developed to address such issues. What's more, we want to share with you some stories about places where ordinary religious leaders, lay and clergy together, have faced such issues. These stories describe what the issues were, what they decided to do about them, how they did it, and what happened as a result.

Welcome aboard!

### Checklist 1: Focus on Congregations

Take a few minutes to review this list of challenges and hold it up against the life of the group of which you are a leader. Make a check in the space provided to the left if in your opinion the challenge is one you are facing at this moment.

     1. Many of our members seem unclear about what we are all about, what we stand for, what our mission is.

     2. Our educational programs are not designed for adults who want to engage in serious learning about being disciples.

     3. Some of our members think the congregation needs a vision for the future.

     4. In the past few years, we have been losing more members than we are gaining, and we are unclear about how to attract new members.

     5. Demographic changes have occurred in our neighborhood.

     6. We have an aging congregation, and many of our biggest donors are in their sixties and seventies.

     7. In our congregation we don't seem to be "connected" to one another as we used to be.

___ 8. We do not feel very connected to our regional and national offices.

___ 9. Money is a big worry, and we regularly defer maintenance on our building and grounds, as well as short-change administrative support.

___ 10. To tell the truth, we don't relate much to other congregations of our own denomination—much less to others.

___ 11. We have a hard time recruiting, motivating, and training new leaders for our key committees.

___ 12. We do not talk about controversial issues, even important ones.

___ 13. Our outreach and mission work is not as strong as it used to be.

___ 14. Our worship life needs to be enriched. We keep hearing "same old, same old" about worship.

___ 15. We need to attract younger people and families.

___ 16. We are not keeping abreast of new technologies that might enhance our worship services, administration, and outreach.

___ 17. We have difficulty accepting change.

If you have checked even one of these 17 items, you have identified a challenge that the rest of this book will help you explore and address.

Next, go down the left margin (right next to your check marks), and indicate with an asterisk all the issues you consider seriously troubling. If you like, use two, three, or even four asterisks to indicate the intensity of your concern.

Now look at appendix A in this book. You will find a clean copy of this checklist also available on the webpage for this book at www.alban.org. Make enough copies for each board member, and take the copies to the next board meeting and have members fill them out. Then discuss the similarities and differences you find among your responses. Allow lots of time to talk about the checklist. You may even find it helpful to break the board into groups of three or four for the discussion.

### Checklist 2: Focus on Religious Institutions
The following list of issues is for people who serve in theological seminaries, judicatory offices, and other religious non-parochial organizations. If that's where you spend most of your time, these questions may help you discover areas in which you may need to consider change.

Make a check in the space provided to the left if you think this issue is a real concern for your institution.

__ 1. Membership losses worry us. Membership is slipping, and contributions that sustain our work are diminishing.

__ 2. Population changes complicate our life. We need to be active and visible in areas where we are not; and we need to pick up our tents and pull out of some areas where we are currently working.

__ 3. The sense of connection has eroded within the organization, among people in the various geographic areas we serve, and between the organization and those whom we serve.

__ 4. Money is a worry.

__ 5. Our relations with other regions and our national office are not very useful or satisfying.

__ 6. We operate as if we were in separate silos, with very little sense of the whole. People work in their departments on their piece of the action, at times unrelated to what others are doing, or to the overall vision. Horizontal communication is poor.

___ 7. We do not know whether we are serving the needs of our constituents.

___ 8. Volunteers are hard to recruit and even harder to motivate.

___ 9. Professional development, if it happens at all, is self-directed, with no consideration of the leadership needs of the whole.

___ 10. We often spend inordinate amounts of time on parts of the system that are not functioning well, neglecting the healthier parts.

___ 11. We need to develop programs and educational systems that will help both clergy and laity in our changing world.

___ 12. We don't keep up with or use technology well.

___ 13. People in our organization are polarized about change, with some championing the need for change while others want to keep things as they are.

If you have checked even one of these issues as a current concern of your organization, you may find it helpful to check your impressions with those of others—your board, faculty or key division leaders, or staff people. Appendix A and the Alban website provide clean copies of this checklist, so you may copy and distribute it to others and see how they perceive these issues—how they confirm what you think and how they may differ.

# Chapter 2
# You Don't Have to
# Do It Alone

IN THIS BOOK, WE ADVOCATE AN APPROACH CALLED "LARGE GROUP Methods" as an invaluable way for faith-based organizations to work with the complex challenges they face. Large Group Methods have to do with getting all the stakeholders together to work on major issues of common concern. These methods differ from the more traditional approaches in which a representative executive group makes the decision and then communicates it to the congregation. In those meetings the congregational members are seated auditorium-style, and while there may be questions, the congregation is not involved in any significant way. The methods we explore in this book are based on the concept that it may take the whole organization to revitalize the congregation or institution. As religious bodies address the challenges of today's environment, there is a need not only for expertise, but also for ownership of the issues, creative ideas for generating change, commitment to the future, and a different way of managing.

These requirements add a new dimension to the leadership role. The leadership task is to know when an issue would benefit from gathering all the "stakeholders" in the room. Our goal in this book is to provide an understanding of the scope and characteristics of Large Group Methods, as well as an understanding of when they may be most helpful. Chapters 4 and 5 contain descriptions of situations in which these approaches have made a significant difference in congregations, seminaries, and judicatories. The term "Large Group Methods" encompasses a series of approaches that, as Marvin Weisbord and Sandra Janoff, originators of one of them, Future Search, put it, "seek to get the whole system in the room." This method is in contrast to small-group methods familiar to faith-based communities. Small groups generally come together to accomplish concrete or specific tasks: congregational governance, community outreach, educational programming, spiritual reflection, and so forth. Their work may be communicated in a bulletin, as a report, at a general meeting, or not at all.

You might wonder whether it is inefficient and unproductive to ask more than ten or twelve people to explore an issue and to make decisions. Certainly, involving more people can be time-consuming and more complicated to manage. There will always be situations in which a small group or governing board might be more efficient and effective in making decisions. But in other situations the Large Group approaches unquestionably yield the greatest overall efficiency. The nature of the issue that needs attention dictates whether a large group—that is, a whole system—approach will be more effective than the efforts of a smaller group. Two important characteristics distinguish Large Group Methods from the efforts of a small group or an executive team to wrestle with an issue. First, as we have mentioned, Large Group Methods seek to gather all the stakeholders, not just the decision makers. Second, the Large Group Methods are highly participatory and democratic. You want to have the decision makers in the room, but you also want to have other people with expertise, the people who do the work, and those who will be responsible for implementing the solutions. You are creating an environment in which each of these groups is fully heard. In the case of a faith-based community, the *internal* stakeholders would be the entire congregation and its leaders: youth director, music director, pastor, teachers, and the like; but the stakeholders might also include outsiders, such as a judicatory representative, leaders from community agencies with which the congregation works, or representatives from the community. The choices depend on the purpose of the gathering and the extent to which outside stakeholders might add perspective and support, or even financial contributions.

Before we describe the methods that are being used by many faith communities today, we ask the most important question: "Why?" Why on earth would you want to involve the whole congregation, and even some external stakeholders, in a strategic planning process or in a session to discuss an important issue? It is an essential question to ask. As the saying goes, "You really oughta wanna."

First, we offer an example of the business application of Large Group Methods. A furniture manufacturer was having trouble with its distribution network. It was not clear where in the process the most important problems were originating. In determining who should attend a meeting to improve distribution, the executive group decided to include all employees who worked in distribution, as well as people from marketing, sales, and IT (information technology). In addition, the executives involved their suppliers and customers. All those groups, whether external or internal, had a stake in the issues. The company knew that if it was serious about improving the distribution of its products, it had to get help from the people who sold the product, the people who bought the product, the ones who made it, and even the people who drove the distribution trucks. Each of these could bring knowledge, experience, and important perspectives to the issue being discussed. Large Group Methods were the efficient alternative for this company, because everyone involved in the process needed to be in the conversation, not just the executive team. Getting the "whole system in the room" was the only way the company could uncover the core issues and develop a comprehensive solution. One discovery was a problem in the order entry system, which was subsequently redesigned. In another instance, the problem was not in the manufacturing but in the packaging.

Under what circumstances would you engage the whole system in a faith-based organization? Here is an example from Billie's conversation with a pastor who was concerned about a critical choice facing his congregation. Billie was attending a dinner party at a friend's house; her dinner partner was the pastor of a church in another state. As they chatted and he discovered that Billie had done some consulting with faith-based communities, he started to describe a situation he was facing with his church board. The board was at odds about a property next door that had become available for purchase. The congregation was growing, had a large Sunday school, and needed more space for expansion. The older board members were reluctant to take on more debt or to burden people with a capital campaign. "The debate breaks down along generational lines," he said. Here is how the conversation went:

*Billie*: This sounds like an important decision with implications for the future of the church.

*Pastor*: Absolutely. As you can tell, I think this is a risk worth taking, but I understand where some of my older board members are coming from.

*Billie*: Why don't you involve the whole congregation in this decision? There is a saying that "people will support what they help create."

*Pastor*: I would be very concerned about involving the whole congregation. That could be chaotic. It could split the congregation.

*Billie*: You know, there are some methods being used today that minimize conflict. They combine the use of both small and large groups. Small mixed groups of about six to eight people explore the issue and hear the different perspectives. Since we tend to hang out with people who view the world as we do, this mixed group permits multiple perspectives and an appreciation of other points of view. You might have some of the parents of your young people sitting with older parishioners, and eight o'clockers mixed with ten o'clockers. You might even ask some of the teenagers to attend and put them in different groups mixed in with the adults. These mixed groups handle differences very well, and they begin to understand the other perspective.

*Pastor*: It would be very positive to have people meet each other across some of these boundaries. What else happens?

*Billie*: Some of these methods are like a strategic planning process. In the situation you are describing, you might want to start first by depicting a history line on the wall. What has been happening to the town in the past twenty years? On another history line you would show what has been happening with the church in the same time period. That would put the issue of the property in a historical context. The congregation could develop these timelines. There are other activities you could do, but at some point you would want to ask people about the future they desire for the church. "What would we like to see happening five years from now?"

*Pastor*: This is an interesting idea. I think it would be important to see the purchase of this property in a larger context. I would need, of course, to have my church board agree to something like this.

At the end of the evening Billie recommended a colleague, who lived in the pastor's state, as a consultant to the church on the use of a method that would encourage congregational participation in the decision-making process. A few months

later Billie learned that the congregation had been very successful with the use of a Large Group Method, and a unanimous
decision had been made to buy the property. An extraordinary
thing happened a few days after the Large Group event. A rela-
tively new member of the congregation was so excited about
the meeting that he gave a large sum of money toward the
purchase of the property. The pastor was pleased that people
had the opportunity to meet one another across generational
and other boundaries, observing, "It developed a whole new
sense of community and ownership." The pastor also commented, "The board and I recognized that we cannot run this
church in the same old way."

In our research for this book we talked with pastors, church
leaders, and rabbis who have used Large Group Methods and
asked them to tell us about their experiences. Here are some
of the responses we heard:

> I have used these methods when there is an important is-
> sue that needs to be addressed by the whole congregation.
> I ask myself, Does this change require commitment and
> wisdom from everyone? If the answer is 'yes,' we involve
> everyone.
>
> *A rabbi*

> These methods create broad ownership of the issues and
> generate creative ideas, support for action steps, and finan-
> cial commitment.
>
> *A United Church of Christ pastor*

> The bishop was about to close our doors. But we used a
> Large Group Method with the whole congregation, we
> renewed ourselves and our commitment, and raised three
> million dollars, and we are thriving today. The long-term
> impact was that it changed the way we work together.
>
> *A United Methodist pastor*

We run our parish using one of the Large Group Methods. With the shortage of clergy, we want our parish to be less authority-dependent and get everyone to take responsibility for the church. This is how we operate.

*A Roman Catholic priest*

In summary, we would say that Large Group Methods are useful because they:

- Create broad ownership of issues and challenges facing the institution.
- Allow people to hear different perspectives on issues, and to learn from each other.
- Use the wisdom and experience of the whole gathering.
- Help people feel valued and efficacious (they have a "voice").
- Change perspective from a self-centered focus to the larger community: you can hear conversations move from "my" and "me," to "our" and "we." This shift helps build a sense of community.
- Have the potential to align the whole system around a future direction or change.

We encourage you to consider these approaches to change. They have helped other faith-based communities face today's challenges. There is something very powerful in gathering both internal and external stakeholders and saying to them, "Come now, let us think about this together" (Isa. 1:18).

The following chapter provides an overview of Large Group Methods, while chapters 4 and 5 include stories from a variety of congregations and institutions that have used these methods in their efforts to bring about change. You may want to move directly to those accounts, but exploring the methods first will, we believe, help you better understand the stories. You can, of course, move back and forth. Enjoy your exploration of this book.

# Chapter 3
# Methods That
# Generate Change

In *THE HANDBOOK OF LARGE GROUP METHODS* (JOSSEY-BASS, 2006), Billie and her colleague Barbara Bunker identified fifteen Large Group Methods that had emerged in the previous ten years. They categorized the methods under three headings: those that engage people in creating the future together, those that address issues around work design, and those that primarily generate discussions.

These methods, even though they may be used for diverse purposes and contain different activities and exercises, are similar in their underlying core principle. Today, people who use these methods in working with organizations often combine and adapt them to meet the organization's specific needs. We call this the "Hong Kong tailor" approach, as the method is custom-designed for the situation, just as a Hong Kong tailor cuts a suit to the specific needs and measurements of the customer. The customization or "cut-and-paste" approach is in fact increasingly becoming the norm with these whole-system-in-the-room methods as they are applied to a wider variety of highly complex challenges. The consultant and the planning team work together to assess the needs of the institution, selecting and combining the Large Group Methods that will be most helpful, given the organization's characteristics and the desired outcome for the meeting.

We have chosen four of these methods to describe in this book—two that are useful for creating a desired future and two that are useful for discussion and exploration of important issues. We selected these four methods because they have helped many religious institutions manage change, plan a preferred future, and address vital issues.

This book is not meant to be a how-to volume; it is not a guide on how to design and run a large-group change event. Our primary purpose is rather to familiarize leaders—clergy, lay, judicatory, and seminary—with these whole-system approaches and to provide a conceptual framework for evaluating their potential usefulness against any given challenge. Our goal is to give enough detail to provide the reader a solid grounding in how these processes work. In chapters 4 and 5 we describe how these methods have been used to address some of the challenges identified in the surveys in chapter 1. Finally, in the resource section of this book we provide a list of books that describe in detail the design and facilitation of these methods.

## Core Elements of Large Group Methods

All four methods establish a climate necessary for Large Group events to be effective by:

- Breaking through the usual institutional silos, cliques, and hierarchies
- Leveling the playing field
- Giving people a voice
- Setting up processes for conversations that make a difference

These approaches develop energy and commitment across the system. The core elements of most of them include:

1. A clear purpose statement
2. Stakeholder inclusion
3. Interactive processes around concrete tasks appropriate to the purpose of the gathering
4. Exploration of the institutional and external contexts before decision and action
5. Self-managed small groups
6. Focus on a preferred future and common ground
7. Responsibility for action by participants

The following section is a description of each of these core elements and why they matter.

## 1. A Clear Purpose Statement

Purpose is important to an organization's effectiveness. Peter Drucker, author and management consultant, would always ask his clients, "What is the purpose of this organization or this meeting?" It is a great question. In consulting it is called "the big why." If a congregation or organization is considering using a Large Group Method, the primary question to ask is this: "Why do we want to have this meeting?" The planning committee and the board are usually responsible for this first step. Here are some important questions to ask:

- Why do we want to bring people together?
- Why is it important to involve more people?
- What are the outcomes we would like to see?
- What would make the meeting important to the people who come?
- How can we frame the purpose statement for this gathering in a *compelling* way, so that people will knock the doors down to come and participate?

## 2. Stakeholder Inclusion

As we have mentioned, the fundamental intent of any Large Group Method is to "get the whole system in the room." How you map the scope of the system is vital to the process. Russell Ackoff at the Wharton School at the University of Pennsylvania, an expert on systems theory, would ask his classes, "If you want to improve public school education in your community, where do you start: the local school, the school-district level, the state department of education, the PTA, the teachers' union, the taxpayers' association, the university school of education, or the students?"

In faith-based communities, determining who should be at the table is also important if you are planning a gathering to renew the congregation, change the seminary curriculum, or wrestle with challenges affecting the organization. It is useful to go back to the purpose statement and ask, "Given the purpose of this meeting, who are the people who have a stake in this issue? Who can contribute to our thinking? Who can bring expertise and experience?" The best way to do this is first to list the categories of people you want representation from: committees/departments, institutions, and agencies you work with, and other important groups. Then brainstorm about the people from each category who might be most helpful, given the issues to be discussed. This list might include those who:

- Care about this issue
- Are the decision makers or have the authority to make decisions in their area
- Have special knowledge and expertise
- Provide support necessary to move ahead
- Are responsible for implementing decisions
- Have diverse viewpoints
- Will be affected by decisions that are made

- Are potential blockers but may become allies
- Others?

## 3. Highly Interactive Processes

These methods use several types of groupings in one large room. The idea of the "system in the room" is supported by seating small groups at five-foot round tables. These small groups provide for more intimate interactions among participants, and the small group allows more "air time" for people to express their ideas. This arrangement is in contrast to the frequent use of breakout rooms at many conferences. The problem with breakout rooms is twofold. Time is lost in traveling back and forth between the breakout room and the main room, and the sense of the "whole system in the room" engaged in the same task, an important element in these gatherings, is missed when breakout rooms are used. In two of these methods, Future Search and the Appreciative Inquiry Summit, all the groupings listed below are used. Open Space and World Café make use of self-selected small groups, and only reporting occurs in the total group.

- The total group
- Small max-mix groups
- Homogeneous groups
- Self-selected Groups

### Total Group

Small groups will report out to the large group, and then all will reflect on what they are hearing. In the large group people deepen their understanding of the whole, build on ideas, and address issues. It is in these discussions that people discover new opportunities across the boundaries of experience, perspective, and role. Activities such as creating timelines and mind maps of external trends are all done in the total group.

## Max-Mix Groups

Table groups are composed of six to eight people. You will want a maximum mix at each table. First, think about the diversity in the congregation and the community. The stakeholder list will help. You will want a microcosm of the whole at each table, a mix of outside and inside stakeholders.

In these mixed groups major work gets done and important conversations take place. As people hear different perspectives, their understanding of the issues is enriched, divergent opinions come together, and people start building on one another's ideas. A curious thing can happen in these groups: people may build relationships across the internal/external boundaries as well as develop new relationships within the community. Sometimes, for the first time, people experience that they are part of a larger whole. These max-mix groups are another place where conflict is constructively managed and common ground is found.

## Homogeneous Groups

This type of group is useful for getting the perspectives of a specific stakeholder group or a work group on a given topic or a contemplated change. Such groups might include the outreach committee, the education and program committee, the activities group, and the alumni or faculty group. Homogeneous stakeholder groups are also useful for planning, implementation, and follow-up.

## Self-selected Groups

People are not assigned to these groups but choose to join them. The members will have one characteristic in common: they are all interested in carrying out some specific action. So in that way, the group might be thought of as homogeneous. The basis of these groups is people's specific interest. They are formed when a particular activity or topic needs attention and some of the community members feel drawn to work in that area and carry the idea forward. At times, after the event, these self-selected groups carry over and continue to work in the organization on the specific issue they care about.

## 4. Exploring the Context First

Before participants get engaged with the issues and challenges in the current situation, they are asked to step back and see the situation in the context of both the organization's history and the history of what has been happening in the external environment in the world. Recognizing the impact of the congregation's history as well as the forces in the current external environment creates a shared context for addressing the challenges. It helps people recognize that "we're all in the same boat." It moves people from focusing on pet solutions and personal agendas to developing a deeper and broader understanding of the situation. There is a movement from "me and my agenda" to "we and the work we need to do together."

## 5. Self-managed Small Groups

The facilitator or consultant usually gives the instruction and the time frames for each task from the front of the room. The facilitator will also remind the group of the listing of guidelines for good conversations that have been placed on each table in addition to instructions to assist the groups in self-management. In most of these methods the small groups self-manage, rotating the leadership roles of facilitator, recorder, and reporter for each assignment. Each group is provided with a guide to performing the group leadership roles. In addition, each person has a packet of instructions for each activity.

Self-managed groups give people voice and opportunity to exercise influence. The rotation of the various roles in the group and the guidelines for good conversations expose people to effective ways of working in groups and running meetings. This training carries back to the institution.

## 6. Focus on a Preferred Future, Finding Common Ground

The focus in these meetings is not on fixing past problems. The challenge for the participants is to create the future they want while building on the strengths already present.

We bring to most strategic or task-related gatherings our own views on what needs to be done, our ideas of how to fix things, and our own agendas. As these meetings progress and people come to understand the larger environmental context and the desired future, a convergence takes place. Divergent points of view are integrated into a shared perspective. People begin to let go of pet solutions. Participants find common ground. Rather than spending hours trying to fix the present, the group finds that the future becomes a compelling force and motivator to work together toward that future.

## 7. Participants' Responsibility for Action

Once there is agreement on the desired future, the community can organize itself and take responsibility to accomplish the action steps required to move toward that future.

In the following section we will describe the four approaches we selected. After each pair we will add our own thoughts and reflections on their use.

# Creating the Future Together

The two methods that follow are generally used for strategic planning: Where are we? Where do we want to go? What action do we need to take to get there? Chapters 4 and 5 include

# Methods for Creating the Future Together

| FUTURE SEARCH<br>*Marvin Weisbord and Sandra Janoff* | APPRECIATIVE INQUIRY SUMMIT<br>*David Cooperrider* |
|---|---|
| Purpose: Search a preferred future | Purpose: Builds future on recognizing and expanding existing strengths |
| • Set format explores past, present, future, and action planning | • Format similar to future search |
| • 18 hours over three days | • May be done over several days |
| • 40–150 or more participants, adjustment needed for additional participants | • Number of participants is unlimited |
| • Stakeholders participate, no experts | • Includes stakeholders |
| • Exploration of external context prior to decision making and action | • Four phases: |
| • Minimizes differences, searches for common ground | — Discovery: Interviews and storytelling surface positive strengths |
| • Self-managed small-group and large-group discussions | — Dream: Based on stories and interview data, group builds a desired future |
| • Action planning groups for follow-up | — Design: Addresses the system changes needed to support the desired future |
| | — Delivery: Implementing and sustaining the change |

examples of both Future Search and Appreciative Inquiry. One example of the application of Future Search is the story of Virginia Theological Seminary in chapter 5. An example of the use of the Appreciative Inquiry Summit is found in the story of the Society of the Sacred Heart in chapter 5 as its members address the changes needed for the future.

The chart on page 25 is just a snapshot of both methods showing the flow of events.

## Future Search

Marvin Weisbord and Sandra Janoff developed the Future Search process. It builds on the work of other people in the field of Organization Development and follows the core elements listed above. It is an approach widely used by for-profit and not-for-profit organizations, NGOs (nongovernmental organizations), and faith-based communities in many areas of the world. One of the authors of Future Search has used it on every continent except Antarctica. It accommodates forty to eighty-plus participants, and in its original form, it takes eighteen hours and is usually held over two and a half days. Billie has applied it with 250 participants, but certain modifications are necessary to maintain effectiveness with so large a group. The flow during a two-and-a-half-day process looks like this:

- Focus on the past: What is our history, how did we get here?
- Focus on the present: What are the current trends that are having an impact on us?
- Taking responsibility—"Prouds and Sorries": How are we responding to these trends and how do we want to respond in ways that we are not responding now?

- Focus on the preferred future: Five years from now, what is happening in our congregation that excites us? What activities are going on? What changes are we seeing?
- Action planning: Once the scenarios of the future have been agreed upon, important questions remain: What do we need to get there? How do we need to organize to accomplish this? What is our time frame? How will we monitor our progress?

An important element in Future Search is the external environmental scan, even when the group is working on its history, which usually includes at least three or four timelines. As members of the congregation or religious institution note the major events and milestones in its history, they are also noting what was happening in the external environment, the world, the town, and even in participants' personal lives during the same period of time. How have the changing demographics of the town affected us? Has the growing polarization in the larger society touched us?

A Future Search was recently done in what had been a large, flourishing congregation. The town had boomed during World War II, when a large manufacturing plant provided employment and contracts with many small businesses in the community. Then tragedy struck: a few years after the war, the plant was closed. Several of the outside stakeholders—including the mayor and the superintendent of schools—and many of the congregation's members described the consequences. Young people left the town to find jobs, property values crashed, the demographics of the population changed, school enrollment dwindled, town revenues declined, and the church lost many of its members. At some level, people knew this, but seeing the town history in conjunction with the church's history helped the congregation face up to the issues and take proactive steps for the future of the church and its members.

Once the history has been completed, the group moves to the *mind map*, which focuses on the present. Several large sheets of easel pad paper are hung together on a wall, and the congregation's or institution's name is written and circled in the center of the papered area. Current environmental trends having an impact on the institution are then called out by the group and listed as lines coming into the center and touching the organization. The implications of these trends for the congregation's or organization's future are then explored.

The second step in examining the present is focusing on the congregation or organization. Those present are asked to review the history and the current external reality in relation to the organization and to reflect on "prouds"—what they have accomplished, what they are proud of, and what their strengths are. This is an affirming process, acknowledging the building blocks that exist for the future. This exercise is followed by naming what are termed "sorries"—people take responsibility for what they are sorry about in relation to the congregation or institution. The participants acknowledge what they have "done or left undone," what has been neglected, mistakes that have been made. This owning up and taking responsibility has a salutary effect: it allows the group to move on. It has a liturgical flow; we rejoice and we acknowledge our failures. Then the small groups are asked to list what they wish they had done, what should have been addressed.

From this point, Future Search participants move on in mixed groups to create a preferred future for the organization. The ideas from the small groups are often presented in creative ways: skits, TV talk-show interviews, a news report from the future, and so forth. The group then identifies common themes in the preferred-future scenarios, and when agreement emerges, they begin planning for action by reflecting on the question, "What steps need to occur to actualize the desired future?" Small task groups are formed to address these questions and plan the implementation. Follow-through is essential!

## The Appreciative Inquiry Summit

The Appreciative Inquiry Summit approach is a hybrid method that has its origin in the Appreciative Inquiry (AI) method created by David Cooperrider and his colleagues at Case Western Reserve University. It was initially developed purely as a data-gathering method. Trained interviewers collect stories and examples that emphasize the strengths or life-giving qualities of an organization or community. Unlike most surveys, which focus on weaknesses or deficiencies in the organization or community, David Cooperrider et al. propose data-collection questions that take an appreciative rather than a critical stance. They ask people for examples of the best in the organization or situation, prompting them with "What do you most appreciate about this community? Tell me a story about this community that exemplifies this quality." This is a reframing process. Rather than ask, "What don't you like about this community?" the interviewer would rephrase the question and ask, "What more would you like to see in this community? If this community was working at its best, what would be happening?" These questions expand the interviewees' horizon about what might be possible, and help them to envision a future they would want.

The Appreciative Inquiry Summit (AIS) method combines Appreciative Inquiry with a large-group methodology called the Summit Meeting, which is similar to Future Search. True to its values, though, the Appreciative Inquiry Summit focuses only on the positive in all the phases of the summit meeting. Large Group Methods in general do not belabor problems;

the focus is on creating the preferred future. Nevertheless, the AIS orientation is even more positive than others.

The reframing process, which is integral to the AI approach, does not permit issues to be expressed in deficit terms. One would not say, "We don't have young people in our congregation," but would rather ask, "What can we do to attract more youth to our community?" This type of reframing leads to more creative and innovative approaches. The group, rather than bemoaning or blaming, suggests new approaches and change strategies for creating a new future. When considering this approach, however, it is worth thinking through whether "owning" past omissions and errors might also be a productive step for the participants.

A unique aspect of the Summit Meeting is that it always starts with appreciative interviews. There are various ways this happens, but the core task is to help people discover their congregation or institution at its best. There are usually four phases in the meeting: the Discovery Phase, the Dream Phase, the Design Phase, and the Delivery Phase. Here is a brief description of each phase.

## 1. The Discovery Phase

The first steps in the Summit meeting are the appreciative interviews around the conference theme. These interviews are conducted in pairs, either before the meeting or as the initial activity of the event. The task of the interviewer is to draw out the core elements in the community that are positive and life-giving. During this Discovery Phase, stories and examples are shared, highlighting those elements that give life and meaning to the congregation or institution. Interviewers often tell the stories, or the stories are collected and people have the opportunity to read them. The total group participates in creating a core map listing the strengths, resources, values, and unique capabilities within the congregation.

## 2. The Dream Phase

The positive elements collected from the interviews, the examples, the wishes, and the dreams are developed into possibilities for the future. People in the total group are invited to envision the institution five or ten years hence, living out its full potential, and to create, much as in a Future Search, a vision for that future.

## 3. The Design Phase

The Design Phase is the part of the Summit Meeting that follows the Dream Phase. The task now is to examine how to align the parts of the organization, so that they are "lined up" to support the articulated future. Does our infrastructure support our new vision? This task requires examining committee structures, policies, systems, and the current organization and asking the tough questions: Does the current way we operate support the future we want? What needs to change? This is the action-planning section. It is an important phase, but it is too often left to the end, when there is insufficient time to fully address it. We know several religious institutions that have carried out this activity several days later, dedicating a full day to this process. This part could happen either as part of the original summit or several days later. The idea is to first create an overall view or "rendition," as architects call it, of the future and then to return to build the structure that will enable it.

## 4. The Delivery Phase

This section is about how to sustain and nurture change. Certain questions need to be explored and reiterated continuously as implementation moves ahead. How are we going to sustain and nurture this new direction over time? Are we taking the necessary actions in a timely fashion? How are we going to incorporate and socialize new members into this new and appreciative way of working?

## Our Reflections on These Methods

There is a different emphasis in each of these methods. Appreciative Inquiry puts front and center a positive framework and keeps the focus there. This approach helps participants recognize:

- The inherent strengths in the institution.
- The positive core in the congregation or organization.
- A new sense of community as they share their appreciative stories with each other.
- A foundation for the future in the building blocks that are already present.
- The reframing process around issues of concern that generates creativity and new approaches to addressing challenges.

In contrasting these two methods, we note that Future Search puts more emphasis on examining the context of the congregation or organization—using the history time lines and exploring the trends that affect the organization in the present. These activities can be very informative. The analysis of the context can provide stimulating insights. We see it as part of the discovery process and believe that these activities are particularly important for religious institutions. They are listed in some of the AI Summit literature as "optional," but we strongly recommend their inclusion.

There is another activity in Future Search that focuses on the present. During this activity people at their tables articulate what they are proud of having accomplished, given challenges they have faced, and the "sorries," described in the description of Future Search—an acknowledgment of issues not addressed.

We do not see this as deficit thinking but as a recognition that something important was ignored, a difficult issue was not faced, the focus was inward rather than outward, or no one stepped up to the plate and took appropriate action. We see this as a salutary process, because it fosters acknowledgment, owning up to what has happened and not happened, and leads to taking more responsibility for the future.

In the Design phase of the Appreciative Inquiry Summit, we like the explicit naming of the elements that may need to change or be added to forward the "Dream." "Do our structures, committees, policies, procedures, and leadership style support our new direction?" "What needs to change or be added?" Once a new direction is set for the institution or congregation, the alignment of the infrastructure to that new vision and purpose is essential.

We suggest combining these two methods. Prior to the large-group gathering, appreciative interviews can be conducted that focus on the strengths of the congregation or institution. Results of these interviews can be reported at the start of the gathering. We also suggest using the history exercise, the mind map of current trends affecting the institution, and the activity called "prouds" and "sorries." This combination would use the best of both methods.

## Exploration and Discussion

Open Space and World Café are excellent methods for connecting people in the congregation or organization. They also take the lid off the box; they free people to speak up in a way that does not happen in regular congregational meetings. Since this book is about change, we believe this is one of the ways that the whole issue of change can be explored without any pressure to make decisions. In chapter 4 there is an example from St. Peter Lutheran Church (Missouri Synod). There the

# Methods for Discussion and Exploration

| OPEN SPACE<br>*Harrison Owen* | WORLD CAFÉ<br>*Juanita Brown* |
|---|---|
| Purpose: A divergent process for purposes of discussion and exploration of issues | Purpose: A process for a group to explore an important issue |
| • Least structured of large-group methods | • Listening to diverse viewpoints and suspending premature judgments is encouraged |
| • One to three days | • Consists of a number of rounds lasting 20 to 30 minutes |
| • Periodic meetings for sharing information across interest groups | • May be done in a half-day to two or three days, depending on issue |
| • Handles over 500 participants easily | • No limit to number of people; more is better than few |
| • Planning group sets theme and determines participants; large group generates the agenda—topics for discussion under conference theme | • Focuses on overarching theme or question |
| • One facilitator lays out ground rules and holds the space | • Large space is set with café tables that seat four people. Tables are covered with butcher paper with markers and crayons available. After each round, three people move to another table, one person remains to host the arrivals from another table. New groups share previous insights and continue exploration. There is periodic community reporting of ideas and insights. |

use of Open Space opened the system to change. The chart here, like the chart on page 25, is just a quick snapshot of the design flow for each of these methods.

## Open Space

Open Space is probably the best known of the methods we are describing in this chapter. Many congregations as well as judicatory bodies have used this method as part of a larger meeting. Several years ago the General Assembly of the Presbyterian Church (USA) invited 500 members to gather before the assembly started and to prepare agenda items with recommendations for later consideration by the delegates to the assembly. The recommendations from this gathering of 500 people were put in book form and given to each delegate to review before the General Assembly.

Open Space has been used with three conservative synagogues around a possible merger, and in numerous other faith-based communities. In our case section (in chapter 4) we will describe some of the uses of Open Space in faith-based communities.

Harrison Owen, an Episcopal priest, developed Open Space. It is the least structured of the methods described here and is reminiscent of an activity often used at conferences called "Free University." At a designated time at a conference, people posted on a wall topics that they would like to teach or learn about with others, and participants signed up to attend the sessions they were interested in. This self-organizing system is not used much today. Open Space is similar. A planning committee picks the theme for the Open Space. The umbrella theme needs to be broad enough to encompass the issues that people would like to discuss with others. Although a broad theme is desirable, it should not be so general that it is amorphous and generates discussions unrelated to the

purpose of the gathering. A church that had moved from an
urban area to the suburbs held an Open Space on the theme,
"How are we doing since the move? What more do we need
to attend to?" Another congregation had as its theme, "What
does outreach mean? What more should we be doing?"

Open Space in its original form brings out issues that
subgroups care about. It is what we call a divergent method,
meaning it bring out lots of ideas. It is expected that people—
either a group or a motivated individual—will subsequently
assume responsibility and take action on key issues. Many
congregations and institutions, however, attach an additional
proactive step at the end of Open Space. We will discuss this
step at the end of these two sections in our reflections on
the two methods. The flow of an Open Space gathering is as
follows.

At the start of the meeting people are assembled in a large
circle. On the floor in the center of this space are large sheets
of paper and markers. The facilitator, after a brief introduc-
tion, reiterates the theme for the meeting and describes these
ground rules:

- Whoever comes are the right people.
- Whenever it starts it starts.
- Whatever happens is the only thing that could
  happen.
- Whenever it is over, it is over. (Thank you, Yogi Berra.)
- The Law of Two Feet applies. *(If individuals find that
  the discussion does not meet their need, they are free
  to go and join another group.)*

The facilitator then invites anyone who has in mind a
topic that fits under the umbrella theme that they would like
to discuss with others to come forward and create the agenda

for the meeting. Participants are asked to pick up a sheet of paper and write the agenda item down and put it up on "The Market Place," a wall set aside for this purpose. Each topic is assigned a space and a time for a meeting. When no more agenda items are offered, people are invited to sign up for those topics they would like to attend and go to the space assigned for that discussion.

Each round of discussions lasts from one to one and a half hours. The initiator of the topic takes responsibility for the discussion of the topic he or she posted as well as for writing up a brief report at the end of the round to summarize the discussion. Depending on the length of the conference, there are usually five rounds in a day, or three in a half-day.

The reports are taken to a location called "The News-room," where they are typed and printed for distribution. This step could also be done in handwriting on sheets of chart paper. The reports are then posted and made available, so that everyone can read about the discussions in each group.

Periodically the group again gathers in a circle for the "Morning and Evening News" to share information across interest groups and to have an opportunity to add new agenda items for people to explore.

As we said, this method is useful in encouraging people to articulate their ideas and thoughts about the theme. We often make assumptions that a governing board or council represents the ideas of the constituents, whereas it may actually represent only its members' own viewpoints. Many congregational members may choose not to be on a board or governing council because their lives are too busy or for other reasons. Nevertheless, they still have ideas, expertise, and commitment. The advantage of this method is that it provides an opportunity for members to identify and talk with each other about areas of common interest or concern.

## World Café

World Café, like Open Space, is intended primarily for exploring an issue, not for decision making or developing a strategic plan. By moving periodically from table to table, people have the opportunity to discuss the theme with a diverse group of people. This method provides an opportunity for people to have meaningful conversations with each other that coffee hours do not provide. It is an excellent way of getting people connected and helps build community.

Juanita Brown, the developer of World Café, uses this informal café-type setting to connect people to ideas and each other, and to have conversations that matter. It can be used for a variety of issues. We have seen it used to explore serious questions in religious settings and to discuss with others a range of topics, such as the decision-making process in an institution, the future of theological education, a biblical passage, and a concern like how to reach out to youth today.

As with the other three methods discussed in this chapter, World Café has a planning group. The planning team begins with the general stated purpose of the gathering and is charged with phrasing the theme or question in a way that will intrigue and draw people to the event. Once the theme or question to be explored is set, the planning group develops stimulating questions for each round to help deepen the conversation on the theme.

The space and decor for a World Café are important. The room is set up and decorated as much as possible to resemble a café. Café-style tables and chairs to accommodate four people per table are arranged around the room. Tables are covered with butcher paper, and crayons and markers are supplied to encourage doodling and note-taking. This sets a more relaxed atmosphere, like a café.

World Café can be done in a half-day, or in two or three days, depending on the question or issue to be explored. We suggest three hours as a minimum. The discussions are usually in three rounds; a half-hour for each round if this is a half-day event. After each round, three people move, each person finding another table to join. One person at each table volunteers to remain as host to welcome the new people who arrive. The job of the table host is to share some of the insights of the previous group and to hear the thoughts of the new group members as they continue to explore the questions. The host also participates in the discussion.

There are no limitations as to numbers, but determining whom to invite is an important task for the planning committee to discuss, given the theme of the conference, because diverse perspectives can enrich the conversations. A host/facilitator introduces the café, the theme, the unfolding of the process, the role of the table host, and his or her own role. The facilitator also explains the principles for good conversations: listening, encouraging others, connecting, and building on each other's ideas.

Usually after the second round, and definitely after the third round, tables report and share with the total group the insights discovered, creative ideas that have surfaced, and recommendations and new questions to be explored. Recorders write on easel pads and capture these ideas, which are then posted on a wall designated for this purpose. Table groups can also write their ideas on sticky-note pads. The sheets are collected, posted on a wall, and similar ideas are clustered together for viewing. The closing activity would be to share what this experience was like for participants, what was learned, and what was stimulated through these conversations.

## Our Reflections on These Methods

These two methods, Open Space and World Café, can be used alone or to engage the community in conversations about various issues of importance. They are effective in creating a sense of community. People get to know each other around conversations that matter and discover common interests.

These methods can also be used as a prelude to a Future Search or an AI Summit. We know one congregation that held an Open Space prior to a Future Search, so that everyone who wanted to have a say could come. The information that came out of the Open Space was then shared at the Future Search event.

We mentioned that these two methods are divergent methodologies; that is, they bring out multiple perspectives that enrich thinking and creativity. They do not include a mechanism to help the entire group find common ground or to set priorities for action. It is assumed that agenda and interest groups will later decide independently to take action based on the gathering's output. Nevertheless, it is worth noting that when either of these methods is used for more than two days, convergence often does occur as people's ideas merge and they discover common ground for action. The reports to the total gathering, whether written or oral, help people recognize areas of importance and agreement. This approach helps the group establish priorities among the different reports, make recommendations, and identify items that require immediate action. The gathered community can then move ahead on setting priorities, assigning responsibility, and establishing reporting methods for follow-up.

We have presented here some of the methods that are being used by faith-based communities today. Currently two Episcopal dioceses are using these methods to address challenges and plan for the future. A Baptist organization focused on reducing poverty is using an AI Summit to plan the extensive work it is engaged in. Chapter 4 tells brief stories about congregations and organizations that have used these methods. In the resource section of this book we have listed books and Web sites that you can explore to learn more about these approaches to change. The point of these methods is that you do not need an expert to come in and recommend changes; in these methods *everybody* improves the system.

# Chapter 4
# Congregational Stories

ONE WAY TO DESCRIBE CHANGE IS TO TELL STORIES. WHAT WE present in this chapter are key moments in several stories—moments that convey the character of change in these religious communities. The whole story of each community would be like a very long movie. One of these stories is much longer than others. The shorter stories are like scenes from the movie—"film clips," as film producers call them. They cover a shorter period of time but help us focus our attention on what is needed for change to take place and illustrate the change process and what can be done to help it happen.

What you see in these stories is how the people in faith communities met a key moment in the life of their organization, broke out of some of the patterns that had previously constrained them, and opened the way to a new future. A story provides a picture of what happened but then allows readers to draw their own conclusions and pull out their own insights. Helpful questions to ask yourself are:

- What are the implications of this story for me?
- What ideas have resonance for the story our community is writing together?
- With whom should I share these stories, this book?

# Envisioning St. Peter's in 2016

St. Peter's is a United Methodist church facing many of the challenges that congregations located in communities of changing demographic circumstances confront today. The story will resonate with many congregations facing similar issues. It is an exciting story of what can happen when people are energized and inspired to work together and create change. It is the longest of the stories, but it gives a very clear description of the steps that need to occur.

## The Background

St. Peter's is located in the heart of Ocean City, an island off the southern New Jersey coast. Methodists founded Ocean City in 1879, and over the years a strong tradition of Methodist values and culture has prevailed in the community. In its glory days there were over 1,200 members in the congregation. For a number of years major meetings of the Methodist Church were held there. Ocean City began to change in the 1980s. Along with many other waterfront communities, it began undergoing a transformation as the baby boomer generation began buying retirement homes in the area. Local real estate prices skyrocketed. Many long-term residents took advantage of this escalation, sold their homes at a nice profit, and moved out of Ocean City to mainland communities. Local school populations declined, and a majority of the high school's students live on the mainland. The age demographics of St. Peter's shifted, and a higher proportion of the congregation's members are now seniors. A number of members have moved into assisted-living facilities on the mainland and can no longer attend services. How to bring them to St. Peter's or how to bring St. Peter's to them has been an ongoing conundrum.

Traffic problems in the summer make commuting on and off the island a problem. Many bridges are in ill repair. Here are some of the challenges that St. Peter's faced that indicated a need for change.

## Challenges

- St. Peter's had a rich heritage and once enjoyed great success. Many people held secret hopes that a miracle would happen and that everything might be as it once was.
- It was an aging congregation. Fifteen to twenty members were in their nineties, and many others were either homebound or in nursing homes. Many members were in their eighties. Handicapped accessibility had long been a concern.
- Stewardship was increasingly difficult. A few of the big contributors had died. Although there was an endowment fund, there never had been a planned-giving strategy.
- The congregation had a tradition of "one large traditional service with classical music." A small group wanted a more contemporary form of worship, and there were indications that a contemporary service might attract more people, but there was no venue for getting this concept discussed.
- Increasingly tight budgets and a perception that attendance was falling off created an unspoken sense of unease about the future of the faith community. As concerns about budget and maintenance increased, administrative issues rose to the top of the agenda. Mission and purpose took a secondary place.
- Some perceived that a small number of "insiders" controlled the agenda. Getting along, honoring the

glorious heritage of the past, and continuing as usual seemed to be the operative norm for some members of the congregation.

- Various small, energetic groups were pushing their own agendas and viewpoints. At one level this was a positive situation, but there was no way to fit these initiatives into a broader purpose, establish common ground, and find agreement on priorities.
- A lack of clarity prevailed about roles and responsibilities.

## What Happened?

The Rev. Brian Roberts had been the assistant pastor twenty years before and was re-appointed to St. Peter's as senior pastor in 2005. In the intervening years, in addition to serving in other churches, he had acquired an MBA degree and had taken courses in organizational development, where he became familiar with Future Search. A year before Pastor Brian returned to St. Peter's, an executive from Dupont, Steve Croft, and his wife retired to Ocean City and joined St. Peter's. Steve had a background in organizational development. Pastor Brian asked Steve Croft to assist in working on a "visioning process." They both felt that this would energize the community. They saw Future Search as a first step, as a catalyst that would generate energy and commitment to a new vision for St. Peter's. Steve wrote, "We knew that the work would go on for several years." Realistically, the "visioning process" was seen as only a first step in a much longer process of managing change.

## The Role of the Board

The administrative board played a supportive role. Board members listened to the description of the proposed visioning weekend meeting. Their decision was to devote $5,000 to the event. (In the end, they came in under budget.) Pastor Brian commented, "They understood the concept of Shared Vision, and that I did not want to lead the congregation where *I* thought God was calling them, but to discern together where we thought God was calling the congregation for the next ten years."

## The Planning Group

A small pilot group of two laypeople and two clergy met initially to discuss the Future Search/Visioning weekend. This group very quickly decided that they needed more people to help plan the event. They drafted nine people from key segments of the community. Pastor Brian and Steve Croft co-chaired the planning group. The first meeting focused on explaining what a Future Search is, the role of the planning team, and issues associated with holding a weekend meeting. The planning group was run as a micro-Future Search. Participants agreed on the role the team should play:

- Understand the event and help fine-tune the design.
- Identify the various constituencies of the community to get all the voices in the room.
- Manage communication to the church at large.
- Make personal contact with the invitees.

One of the first issues the planning group tackled was selecting the theme for the weekend. The theme they decided on was "Rooted in our past, responding to God's call, reaching out for our future." Two biblical quotes were also used to support the theme: Proverbs 29:18 ("Where there is no vision, the people perish" KJV) and Luke 1:37 ("Nothing is impossible with God" NIV).

## Recruitment and Communication

- The planning team developed a list of the positions and people who had to be at the event if the entire system was going to be in the room. Once the list was developed, people were assigned a person to call, or a group or committee to visit to describe the event.

- A letter was sent to the entire congregation inviting everyone to attend. This communication let people know that the weekend meeting was not a "select group" and that everyone was needed and welcome. New people showed up as a result. Planners requested that people make a commitment to attend the entire weekend.

- Announcements were made at Sunday services and included in bulletins and mailings. These announcements were an open invitation to all.

- About 100 key people were sent special invitation letters. Planning team members also made special contact with the key people to identify any barriers to their attendance.

- Arrangements were made for child care to allow parents with small children to attend.

- A major effort was also made to get the youth to attend. About ten of the more active youth came to the event. The views of the youth were an important contribution.

- Those who indicated they planned to attend received a confirmation letter providing details of the event. All who were attending were asked to invest some time before arriving to reflect on St. Peter's and on the following appreciative inquiry questions to help with this reflection:

— What makes St. Peter's special to you?
— Considering your experience with St. Peter's, what nourishes you spiritually and encourages you to follow the path of our Lord?
— Looking ahead, where do you feel God is calling us to serve?
— What would energize and excite you in this regard?
— As you look to the future, what are your hopes and aspirations for how St. Peter's can advance God's work to make a real difference in the world?

Two consultants, members of the Future Search Network who had worked before with congregations, also assisted the planning group. Several weeks before the event the two consultants came to St. Peter's for a day and did a series of interviews with the planning team and other key people. This information gathering and personal contact by the consultants helped cement the planning.

## The Visioning Meeting

The Future Search was held at a conference center near the church and followed the basic steps outlined in chapter 3. Here are some brief notes on the process described by Steve Croft.

> Friday evening we started documenting our heritage; we built time lines that recorded significant events in the lives of our families, St. Peter's, and the world at large. . . . Saturday saw us voicing our concerns over the challenges facing us. We talked and prayed together about these things, and from this shared perspective we began to look to the future. . . . Saturday afternoon eight teams created and then acted out skits depicting their hopes for St. Peter's future. Eight state-

ments were developed from these skits, each depicting some aspect of St. Peter's in 2016. Eighty-plus people attended; they spanned three generations. We worshiped, remembered, planned, prayed, discussed, disagreed, and communed with God and each other. The end result was common ground on a number of areas. . . . No single weekend builds a future, but this weekend helped us get our work started. In subsequent weeks teams formed to undertake the real work of bringing this future to life!

## The Initial Outcomes

The visioning weekend produced a number of action teams that worked together to build a strong foundation for the ongoing revitalization of St. Peter's. The teams were activated around statements that described the congregation—using the present tense—in 2016:

> *Worship Design Team*: St. Peter's offers both traditional and contemporary worship services that are scriptural and Christ-centered.
>
> *Welcoming and Connecting Team*: St. Peter's seeks to connect people to the love of God by welcoming, assimilating, and enabling everyone for ministry.
>
> *Staffing for Service Team*: St. Peter's is staffed to meet the needs of expanded youth and other programs—based on a comprehensive staffing plan.
>
> *Outreach and Mission Planning Team*: St. Peter's is expanding mission and outreach opportunities to increase the congregation's participation.
>
> *Accessibility and Facilities Team*: St. Peter's is handicapped accessible through physical improvements: a new elevator to the sanctuary and the third floor, handicapped-

accessible bathrooms, all based on a master plan and facilities audit.

*Finance and Planning team*: St. Peter's Church is a church that gives to God; 80 percent of the members are now pledging; membership that tithes has increased by 300 percent. Endowments are steadily increasing.

*Technology:* St. Peter's is using newly available technology to keep people connected, to enhance services and programs, and to transcend geographical boundaries, reaching people who do not live on the island.

*Regional Congregation Team*: St. Peter's is providing ministry to the entire region, including tourists and those with second homes. Our youth are able to meet off-island. St. Peter's provides transportation in the region, and we are active in solving traffic and other regional issues affecting St. Peter's.

*Family and Youth Planning*: Youth and families are a rich, dynamic part of St. Peter's ministries. Youth and families are drawn to the church by a wide range of fun, worshipful activities, leaders, and exceptional facilities.

## Sustaining and Nurturing

Follow-up on the visioning work included a number of activities:

- A report to the church was made in a Sunday service.
- An interactive report was given to the administrative board.
- A follow-up meeting was held with families for those who could not attend the April meeting.

- The administrative board began to play a critical role after the visioning meeting, and the board now has a central role in the activities at St. Peter's. It is the place where new initiatives are sanctioned. For example, it approved the funding for the new contemporary service and funding for technology to play an expanded role.
- Progress reports on the Vision have been added to the monthly agenda of the board.
- "Vision leader" is now a standing position on the board, an effort to help keep the focus on the work that needs to be done.
- There have been new infrastructure adjustments to incorporate the new initiatives.
- In a 125-year-old congregation that loves "classical music," there is now a contemporary service, increasing average worship attendance by sixty to seventy people.
- The Welcoming and Connecting team has produced many new materials to use in attracting and assimilating new members.
- St. Peter's services are now being videotaped, the Web site has been upgraded, and soon there will be streaming video available online, so that people can view the service in real time.
- Facilities have been reviewed, and a comprehensive plan will be implemented to revitalize space and accessibility.
- St. Peter's is being actively marketed across the region. Large postcards announcing the new contemporary service were sent to 15,000 people.

## Our Reflections

What helped this congregation make a successful new beginning? The members were blessed to have a pastor who had both initiative and training in large-group methods. They were fortunate that the pastor found a person willing to take a leading role—a layperson with experience from his professional life that matched the pastor's skills. Working together, they got the system in the room. The Future Search method that was used helped the congregation own the need for change and build a vision of the desired future. The group built a team of congregational members and board members and got a nine-member planning group engaged and committed. Early on, the administrative board assisted the initiatives by establishing a calendar and providing financial support. The administrative board also made a commitment to next steps. Initiating a "new service" is a radical effort to bring new life and to test new ideas. The new vision seems to have wide ownership in the congregation.

The leadership clearly recognized that change is a continuous, ongoing process. Future Search was the catalyst; it got everyone "singing off the same page." People recognized differences yet were able to work through these and establish common ground. Future Search alone is not enough. The follow-up mechanisms are the hardest part—adjusting the infrastructure to support the vision, nurturing the initiatives that develop, and keeping the focus. That is what makes the difference in this story.

## St. Peter Lutheran Church (Missouri Synod)

The method used in this example was Open Space—a good method for getting things moving and giving voice to everyone, especially people who are "underheard," as you will see. This is how they dealt with their challenges.

## Background

The pastor had just retired after 33 years of ministry at St. Peter. The congregation was in the doldrums. People had not been initiating many new projects for a few years, and much of what was happening was "going through the motions." Members were leaving; attendance at voters' meetings was down.

Then two events coincided: A new pastor was hired, signaling that something new might happen, and a small group began tinkering with new projects. But something else was needed if the congregation was to say, "We are in charge." A member of the parish, Doug Germann, suggested the use of Open Space as a method that would help identify what was on people's hearts about the work of the congregation in this community. Doug was acquainted with Open Space, having used it for his "community disorganization" work. The pastor signaled a green light. Although the small group that had been promoting new projects was less sure about how this would be received, it summoned the courage to move ahead.

## What Happened?

The theme of the Open Space was "How Then Shall We Serve?" Doug agreed to facilitate the meeting. Everyone was invited to the Open Space, which was announced through the parish midweek mailing and at services. The written invitation described how the Open Space would work. Members were told that everyone was welcome to post and host a breakout session on a topic for which they held some passion and were willing to take some responsibility (if only to host the conversation).

However, the key method for getting people to the meeting was not print materials; it was the hard work of committee members asking people, face to face, to "please come." Several people who had never before been to a congregational meeting came and took strong roles. In the end, every person who was there had been invited by at least one and perhaps by as many as three people, demonstrating that this may be the best way to get people to a working meeting, and maybe the only way.

In our busy society, everyone has more commitments than he or she can possibly keep. Hoping that holding events on a variety of days of the week would give people more chances to come to more of the work sessions (they were encouraged to come and go, even if they could not attend the whole event), planners scheduled the Open Space for 6 p.m. to 8:30 p.m. for four consecutive evenings, Sunday through Wednesday. Child care was arranged. (Paid volunteers were sought from other Lutheran churches in the area so that all members could attend.) Meals were provided; rides were arranged—all without charge or requests for donations. The first three nights were for the Open Space meeting; the second breakout on Tuesday was for action planning; and Wednesday was billed as a "getting-down-to-work session." Each host of a breakout session was given a note-taking form, and the completed forms were collected into the "book of proceedings." The simple format allowed lots of space for answers, including title of session, host, session participants, unanswered questions, summary of conversations, recommendations, ideas, and next steps.

The first evening one woman said, "You know, what I'd like to see is. . . ." She had to be encouraged by people all around the room to post the topic she had raised. She is always in the kitchen and in the background, giving, giving, and seldom speaking. But when she reminded the assembled group that the fellowship hall (a space large enough for about a hundred people at tables for a potluck) had not been painted since the building had been built twenty-six years before, excitement filled the room. The congregation had felt locked into the colors chosen decades earlier by the architect. Now a "we" began to break loose, showing participants that they could do the impossible. By Monday evening, ladders and drop cloths were in the room, and the edging around windows and doors, as well as the baseboards, had already been painted, meaning that there was no turning back. Sunday morning the rest of the parishioners discovered the brightly painted fellowship hall.

This action became a metaphor for what is possible. It was symbolic. Other actions emerged from the Open Space. Votes were not necessary, and no one sought an OK from the church council. Many breakout groups adopted the "we're in charge" attitude and put their ideas into action. For example, the traditional Christmas-basket project was expanded to include Thanksgiving and Easter, following the same families through the seasons. A new over-fifty social group was formed—the Older Wiser Living Saints (OWLS). "Commercials" (announcements for every project going on) after church were dramatically curtailed. Seeds were planted that led to a major overhauling of the constitution a year later. The idea for a demographic study of the neighborhood was planted, to be harvested about two years later.

Less measurable but of perhaps higher significance were the many ways in which people came together when they might not have otherwise. People who favored traditional music and those wanting more contemporary music met to hear each other's heart rhythms and tones. Three moms who seldom had talked with each other huddled for a session on the challenges for parents of middle- and high-school-age girls. Some people flitted like beautiful butterflies without attending a session, but new friendships were kindled. Who can put a number on the value of such fellowship?

Two years after "How Then Shall We Serve," the pastor observed that the opening of space was "permission-giving—it freed people up to feel they can do things without having to jump through eighteen hoops, getting the permission of God and the whole council." A good example of this new sense of freedom is the woman who posted the topic to start the OWLS, a quiet person who spoke softly if at all at voters' meetings. She was able to bypass the council and the voters to start her project. This group is vital and growing two years after the Open Space. Said the pastor: "We were making decisions one way; now we are making decisions another way, too."

As Doug Germann says about the Open Space process, "We do not do these meetings because they change us dramatically. After all, we already had people who were willing to step in. But this event did allow us to catalyze ourselves. We do these things because there is always the possibility that the world might change. This is the biblical definition of hope."

## Our Reflections

Interesting, isn't it—a pastor retires after a long pastorate, a new one is called, and somehow "a small group was tinkering with new projects." Across the country we find that the times when congregations change pastors often turn out to be times when new leaders and new ideas emerge. That clearly was happening here. Not only the "small group" but also a layperson named Doug Germann stepped forward. Changes in pastoral leadership seem to create "open" times for a congregation—times when new enterprises are seen to be possible.

The sense of an open moment seems almost contagious. We hear of people who generally didn't speak up who suddenly seemed to have space and courage to speak up. We (Billie and Loren) were particularly struck by the way the group members took up the idea of painting the room they'd all wanted painted for years. Nobody had stopped them from doing it, but it took this open moment for them to give themselves permission to do it. The fact that a church member knew about "Open Space" gave them a method to work with—and it helped the group members take ownership of their lives and responsibility for their community in a new way. They seem to have expanded their willingness to put forth ideas that they felt would make a difference, or at least to try things they hadn't felt they could try before.

Finally, we wonder, who will help the members keep this climate of openness to try things? Are there new ways they can live together that keep them open to each other and to new opportunities?

# Society Hill Synagogue

This is the story of a very brief event. Like the preceding story, it occurred at a critical time when professional leadership was changing, but this one has a special twist, in that the leader who was retiring was the founder of the community and was leaving with his two professional colleagues who had also had long tenures. Indeed, the three of them had been responsible for establishing many of the core values the congregation had tried to live by. So this moment was key to the community's future identity.

## The Background

The synagogue was founded in the sixties by a very charismatic rabbi. It never affiliated with any of the branches of Judaism—Reformed, Orthodox, or Conservative. At the same time, members had a core of set of values, one of which was a belief in gender equality. The synagogue is located in an affluent area of Philadelphia, and the surrounding community is made up of upwardly mobile professionals. Most but not all members live in the area.

## The Challenge

The rabbi had been the founder of Society Hills Synagogue, and the administrator and the cantor had been a vital and important part of the synagogue for many years. But all three were set to retire. As a member stated, "It was hard to imagine the synagogue without these three people!" Many members of the congregation were dismayed about the announcement and concerned about the future.

The president of the board asked the vice president, Julie Liedman, who then would succeed as president, if she could search for a consultant to help with a strategic plan. Julie, who had a business-journalism background and an in-depth understanding of the synagogue's culture, interviewed several consultants who suggested methods that would take almost a year, but she did not think a long, dragged-out strategic process would work, considering the culture of the institution. Then she spoke to Jean Haskell, an organizational consultant and a member of the congregation, who suggested a shortened version of Future Search. Julie loved the idea and championed it, and the board decided to hold a shortened version of Future Search on a Sunday. Julie thought that this process would give people an opportunity to come together in this period of transition and talk with each other about "issues that mattered for the future."

## What Happened?

Every member of the synagogue was invited to attend, and the planning group agreed to take the first 100 people who signed up. Teenagers were also invited, and some were present. About 60 percent of the congregation members attended.

The Future Search meeting started with Julie introducing the purpose of the conference, which would address the question "Why Are We Here?" The charismatic founder had

articulated the core values, and the congregation had sub-
scribed to them. Future Search would give the congregation
an opportunity to talk together and take ownership of "who
they were, and who they wanted to be" as they created a vision
of the preferred future they desired for the synagogue.

Julie then introduced the two consultants, Jean Haskell
and Gerald Kaufman. Jean Haskell began by describing the
flow of activities they would be following during the day:
"Focus on the past, the present, the desired future, and action
planning." The group started by examining the past, using
three timelines, starting with the founding of the synagogue.
The timelines included Society Hill Synagogue, the world at
large, and the participants themselves on the personal line.
The reflections on the timelines were rich in insights. People
recognized many things they had accomplished, challenges
they had lived through, and core values that were important
to them.

After this activity participants examined the present with a
mind map of the "external and internal trends and issues that
might impact on our future." This activity was followed by
what Jean Haskell calls a "History of the Future." The group
members were asked to imagine that they were at a banquet
to celebrate what they had accomplished at the Society Hill
Synagogue in the previous seven years. Each table grouping
presented its picture of the future. Finally, in the action-planning phase, the group worked on discovering the common
themes in each presentation and planned the appropriate follow-up.

The retiring rabbi who attended remarked at the end that
in the many years he served the synagogue, he had never seen
so many members gather together and not get into an argument. A young man reflecting on the experience said, "In the
years I have attended, this is the first time I have been asked
for my opinion."

## Outcomes

Although participants desired many outcomes, such as more office space and a Hebrew school, they galvanized their energy on developing a profile for the new rabbi, an essential next step. In follow-up discussions Billie Alban had with the president and the consultants, they commented that many members had expressed how meaningful this conference had been and how little opportunity there had been in the past for the members to have a conversation like this. What clearly emerged through these discussions were a sense of identity ("who we are") and an affirmation of the core values that were important to carry into the future. (It is interesting to note that the vision of classrooms for the Hebrew school has now become a reality. An adjacent piece of property became available and was purchased for that purpose.)

## Our Reflections

Once again we run into the issue of "transition." Obviously, turnover of the formal leadership is a threat to the life of such organizations—or at least to the sense of connection and who the congregation is. "Transition" raises the question "Who are we?" so often in groups and communities, because the "official" leader is simply expected to represent and define who the community is. But when that leader leaves, the question comes to the top. Whether people have liked or hated the way the leader has articulated or represented the identity, it comes as a shock when he or she is no longer there. Every group changing leaders feels some of this ambivalence and anxiety. This synagogue (like the Lutheran congregation described above) served itself well to pay some attention to that.

Professionally trained leaders have served each of the three groups we've described so far. In each story, however, key elements in the dramatic changes come from the knowledge and skills of lay leaders—people who bring expertise from their professional areas of responsibility outside the congregation and adapt them for use in the religious community. One suspects that this kind of expertise may be crucial in getting the process of change going and in gaining its acceptance by other members of the community. It is interesting in this case that the vice president of the board was charged with finding a consultant to help with the job—and even to help select the best method. We may need to pay more attention in groups like these to ensure that the way is open for people with skills from outside the faith community to use those skills more readily.

After they had looked at the past, members of the congregation spent time putting themselves into the future, a history of the future. From the vantage point of seven years hence, they looked back and recognized the obstacles they had overcome and what they had been able to accomplish for the synagogue over the intervening time period. The future came to pass.

# First Church of Christ, Congregational

This story relates to a transition, but in this case, the transition had occurred two years earlier, when a new pastor came to First Church of Christ, Congregational, Glastonbury, Connecticut. The new pastor and at least one member of the board decided to try to look at how things were going this early in the pastorate. Again we discover how a talented layperson and a pastor can initiate a congregational effort to look at how change is occurring, if not to initiate change itself. This story also involved the congregation in the decisions to include children and young people in the change effort.

## Background and Challenge

The pastor of First Church of Christ, Congregational, a United Church of Christ congregation, had been there for two years and wanted to hear from the congregation about how things were going. What was the congregation pleased with, and what needed attention? A member of the church council suggested a consultant in the area who worked with both industry and nonprofit organizations and recommended that the consultant be invited to meet with the council to explore the possibility of working together. The consultant described the advantages of using a large-group method that would get everyone involved in exploring the future they wanted for their congregation. She highlighted that this type of participation generates ownership and commitment.

The council contracted with the consultant, who worked with an appointed planning group to design the meeting. The conference-planning group included the pastor, representatives from the congregation, and the chair of the council. The decision was made to use a large-group method involving the whole congregation. A unique aspect was that this event was to include the church-school students or, as someone put it, everyone "from five to eighty-five." An important discussion followed this decision: what to call this meeting? The planners wanted to make it clear that families were invited, but they did not want this to mean that singles were excluded. The decision was made to call this meeting "A Church Family Gathering."

The meeting was similar to a Future Search, although the participants eliminated the history timelines because they had done something similar when they were searching for the new pastor. The conference was about a day and a half, starting Friday at 5:30 p.m. (The excerpt from the planning group's

First Church of Christ, Congregational
Church Family Gathering
DETAILED AGENDA

FRIDAY EVENING

| Time | What | Who | Set up / Handouts | Notes |
|------|------|-----|-------------------|-------|
| 5:30 PM | Moment of Silence | Flo | Meeting House | Handout with several prayers available |
| 5:30 PM | Raggedy Start: Sign in; get nametag with table number on it. Go to big banner and jot a phrase/word/symbol about what you appreciate about First Church. | Noel coordinating traffic flow | Large banner on wall in hall to kitchen. Sign-in sheet used for volunteering later | Tables are numbered. As tables fill in, each group says grace and eats. |
| 6:00 PM | Dinner: During the meal, talk about how you live your faith inside/outside the church. Give examples. | All | Centerpieces with table tent explaining process. Centerpiece questions: "How do you live your faith in the world? Give examples." | Lasagna, salad made by church members |
| 6:25 PM | Group Prayer: Highlight some mealtime conversation (answers to Qs on centerpiece). How do you live your faith in the world? | David | | |
| 6:30 PM | Children Transition | Allison | Big plate of cookies! | |
| 6:30 PM | Where is First Church currently? "Gallery Walk" at 7:00.<br>• What's brought us to this point?<br>• Where are we now?<br>• Where do we want to be?<br>Set context: What works/requires attention? (David) What's been accomplished thus far? (Sarah) Introduce Billie and Anna | Pastor David and Sarah | Reference banner from spring meeting as well as "what we appreciate" banner. | David and Sarah craft talking points and coordinate who covers which points. |
| 7:00 PM | Gallery Walk: One flipchart for each criterion with what works/requires attention positioned around the room. Space available on each flipchart for additions from others. | Billie and Anna | Handout explaining what to do during Gallery Walk. | (1) Read through, then (2) add what most requires attention. |

agenda on page 62 shows how the group laid out its plan for the event.) As people arrived at the church, they encountered just inside the entrance a huge banner of butcher paper about twelve feet long, lots of colored crayons and markers, and a sign inviting them to draw a picture or symbol, or to write a phrase about what they liked most about First Congregational Church. Immediately young and old went to work, adults covering the upper areas and the small kids the lower areas. The activity was great fun, and the banner was then removed and hung in the main room where the congregation would meet. After a spaghetti dinner, the young people went to age-appropriate groups in their classrooms. The adults remained in the large hall. They went through a sequence of steps: what had been accomplished, where they were now, and what areas people felt needed attention.

In small mixed groups people discussed this last question, and each group listed items its members felt were important to address. A sharing of information with the total group followed, duplications were removed, and similar themes were clustered. Each area that needed attention was written up on a separate sheet of easel paper. Everyone was given five blue adhesive dots and one red one. Each person was to place a dot on those items he or she felt were most important; the red dot was for a burning issue that needed immediate attention. The items that received the most dots were reported, and a discussion followed. People were encouraged to reflect during the evening on the areas they wanted to work on the next day. The children's groups arrived from their meeting and presented their hopes for the future, and the evening ended with prayers and a hymn.

Saturday morning started with a prayer and a song. People were encouraged to select an area they wanted to work on and to move to a designated part of the room, so that groups could be formed around areas of common interest. Each work group was given the following list with the task sheet:

1.  If this were happening, what would be going on, what
    would it look like? *Stand in the future and describe
    it.*
2.  What are some of the ways you could see First Con-
    gregational Church achieving this? *Be specific.*
3.  What would we need to make this happen? *Consider
    resources such as time, talent, and treasure.*
4.  What are three concrete steps that are necessary to get
    this started? *Identify specific actions that we would
    take to move this forward.*

The work groups were told that their recommendations
would go to the council to organize and implement. If individuals were interested in working on their group's initiatives,
they were to sign their names to the recommendations, so they
could join the committees that would work on the implementation of these initiatives. A variety of activities for the kids
and young adults focused on the future they wanted for the
church. The teenagers presented a skit of the future they would
like to see. The small children labeled large white cardboard
building blocks with wishes for the church or activities they
would like to see taking place at the church. The blocks were
stacked and built into a church-shaped building to exhibit to
the entire congregation. One group wrote a song, and lots of
pictures were drawn.

## Outcomes

A number of initiatives came out of this event, some focused
on spirituality, others having to do with adult involvement in
mission—more than giving money, actually serving on a mission. New programs for young people were also developed.
Service schedules were changed, and issues about handicapped
access were addressed. The topic of becoming Opening and

Affirming (in some denominations these words mean acceptance of gays and lesbians) was discussed, and the decision was made that First Congregational Church would be known as a church that stood for "equity and social justice" for all. In subsequent interviews people commented, "We see this as a turning point for the congregation," and, "The meeting built a sense of total community we have never had before."

## Our Reflections

The first important point to note is that things were apparently going well in the congregation. This was a checkup; after two years with a new pastor it seemed an appropriate time for such a step. It is valuable periodically to involve the whole system in a process like this.

The title "A Church Family Gathering" is significant, and this story includes a lot of detail of the way the meeting went, especially the appropriate inclusion of the children and young people. We like the way the group used art and other creative activities both to increase the fun of the meetings and to lead to depth about the issues being addressed. Building a model of the church and writing a song sounded like fun and apparently led to significant engagement in the plans for the future.

Several other ideas described should be a resource to anybody working in groups dealing with change. The method of prioritizing with colored dots and the way the "team assignments" are described seem particularly helpful.

# The Merger of Temple Israel and Beth Tikva

Religious groups all over the country, for one reason or another, run into the situation these two synagogues faced.

Sometimes it's that people have moved; sometimes one or more congregations hit a drastic financial crisis; sometimes it's just that there are too many congregations of the same denomination in the area. We have seen situations where there are not enough parking spaces, and there is no place to expand. Downtown property values have so increased in some communities that selling the property and merging with another congregation in another area have become a viable option. It is a difficult decision to pick up your tent, like Abraham, leave everything, and move on. After many years in one place, and many fond associations, weddings, funerals, bar mitzahs, and bat mitzvahs, this is a courageous step. The brief story told here is about two synagogues that proposed and then worked through a formal merger of their congregations to build a new future together.

## The Background

Temple Israel was an older conservative synagogue situated in a downtown area of Washington, D.C. It had a rich history as an important downtown synagogue. At one time it had more than 750 members and a multigenerational congregation. As the demographics changed in the area, the congregation dwindled to fewer than one hundred people. There had not been a bar or bat mitzvah in years. The congregation was made up primarily of older adults.

## The Challenge

Temple Israel members decided to look for another conservative synagogue in another area that they could join. They explored several synagogues in the adjacent region. One of the synagogues they liked was Beth Tikva in Rockville, Maryland, a younger congregation but one with a similar tradition. Representatives of the two congregations met and discussed the possibilities. The president of Beth Tikva had heard about Future Search and talked to Marvin Weisbord and Sandra Janoff about using this method to explore a merger. After further conversations with a planning group that included members of both synagogues, the congregations decided to hold a Future Search Conference, bringing both congregations together. The purpose was to "jointly find a common direction, transition one hundred new members, identify congregational leaders, and talk about the future of the Hebrew school."

## What Happened

The conference was held on a Saturday evening, all day Sunday, and Monday morning into the early afternoon. Stakeholders included:

- Regular members of both synagogues
- Outside colleagues invited as honored guests
- Parents of schoolchildren
- Youth
- Committee members
- Leadership board members
- New members (five years or fewer)
- Supporting members (not active)
- Staff

The Future Search format was followed, beginning with examining the past. A timeline was constructed for each synagogue, honoring the past of each congregation and informing each group about the history of the other. The world and the personal timelines were done, as usual. Exploring the present was done as a joint activity, as was envisioning a preferred future for the one community that was coming into being.

## Outcomes

A number of changes and initiatives came out of this event.

- Today the merged congregation is called Tikva Israel.
- A major building expansion was initiated with the goal of erecting a two-story building that would include more classrooms and a Hebrew school. The congregations raised twelve million dollars for this project.
- A foundation was established called "Temple Israel" for community outreach activities.
- New leadership emerged, reflecting increased participation of the membership.
- The board of directors went from twenty to thirty-six and included members of both congregations, a major factor in the success of the merger.
- The receiving congregation was most welcoming to the new members.
- Temple Israel brought its memorial plaques from the old synagogue, and a room in the new building was set aside to display them.

Ten years after the merger, the current president of the synagogue, Neil Newman, believes that the partnership has been very successful. Many elements contributed to this outcome: the joint planning of the Future Search, the enlargement of the board, and the shared building project, which made it "our synagogue." Money from the sale of the Washington, D.C., property was used to establish a foundation in the name of Temple Israel. The warm welcome given to the members from Temple Israel cannot be underestimated. Neil articulated that using the Future Search process made the difference. "Today we are one," he explained. "You cannot say this person is from there and that person is from here."

## Our Reflections

Neil Newman's "ten-year retrospective" touches many of the
critical events in this effort:

- The congregation that seemed most at risk was
  proactive about its situation. Members decided to look
  for a merger before they used up their resources.
- The planning committee was selected to include
  members of both congregations.
- The combined groups looked at the history of both
  synagogues to get inside the values and the dreams of
  the other, not just their own.
- Many initiatives were taken to include the old within
  the new; setting aside a special place for the memorials
  is one example.
- Care was taken to reach a sense of a "new" beginning
  for both congregations, not just a gluing together of
  two old congregations.

# St. James' Episcopal Church

St. James' is an Episcopal church located in the downtown
area of Danbury, Connecticut. The church is very active in the
community. It holds two services on Sunday, one on Saturday
afternoon, and one during the week. It also maintains an
excellent music program attended by the larger community.
The congregation includes about one thousand individual
members with 460 families. The church dates back to before
the American Revolution, and some members are of the sixth
generation to belong to St. James'. The town at one time was
a manufacturing center for the Northeast. The Congregational
church, which has a similar historic pre-Revolutionary past,
was the congregation of the factory owners and the managers.

St. James', unlike the typical image of an Episcopal church, was the congregation of the people who worked in the factories owned by the Congregationalists. Today St. James' is a middle-class congregation with many members who live in the surrounding towns. When this story took place, there were three ordained pastors—two rectors (a married couple who called themselves "the rector"), who had been there twelve years, and one assistant pastor. St. James' at the time was a healthy and growing parish. The church's environment, however, was changing; large numbers of Latino and Asian families with many social needs were moving into Danbury.

## The Challenge

The vestry (church board) and the rectors decided that it was time to devise a strategic plan for St. James'. What was the future for St. James'? Where was God calling the members?

## What Happened?

The warden (the board chair) approached two management consultants, members of the congregation, and asked if they would work with the vestry to develop a strategic plan. They both said no. The vestry, surprised at this response, offered to change the time of the vestry meetings, assuming that was the issue. The consultants came back and said they would work on a plan only if the development included the whole congregation, because whatever came out of the plan would require the support of the congregation. The vestry agreed to such a process, and a planning team was appointed, including one of the rectors, the warden, and a representative microcosm of the congregation. The consultants described the Future Search process, and planning team members agreed. Knowing what people would like to see five years ahead would be helpful.

Once the recommendation for a preferred future had been developed, the planning team would organize the implementation and regularly report to the congregation on how the implementation was proceeding.

## The Planning Committee

The planning committee decided to post four history timelines—church, Danbury, the world, and personal—prior to the meeting. This exercise allowed members of the congregation to write down, before the conference, the events they recalled on the history lines. Having this done ahead of time saved time in the conference. Some members from the planning committee agreed to visit people in nursing homes or those who were homebound to capture their memories, particularly of the church's history. They also promised those who were homebound that they would be personally informed about the outcome of the meeting.

One of the important tasks of the planning committee is to invite participants. The team needs to make sure that those who attend both represent the congregation and understand the purpose of the conference (in this case, "To develop a plan for the future of St. James': Where is God calling us?"). The St. James' planning committee was successful in recruiting members, and more than 250 people signed up to attend. The group included members from the two Sunday services, external stakeholders, youth, parents of young children, parents of teenagers, seniors, the pastor, the staff, and in general a broad mix of the congregation.

The planning committee developed criteria for external stakeholders to be invited and included a number of people from organizations the church worked with—major social-service agencies, the Dorothy Day Soup Kitchen, and the Women Center (for abused women), as well as a Lutheran pastor, someone from the mayor's office, a representative of the Salvation Army, and the head of the Association of Religious Communities (an ecumenical group that worked together on addressing community issues). Stakeholders were invited both formally (with a letter from the rector and vestry) and in person. The night before the conference, the planning group spent hours putting together the tables of six to eight people who would form the max-mix groups. The conference ran from Friday evening, beginning with supper, through Saturday, including a continental breakfast and lunch. Parking, a big issue for downtown churches, was available. Transportation and child care were provided for those who needed those services. The meeting was held in a large room at the church.

## The Conference

After a general overview of the steps that would take place during the conference and presentation of the roles and norms that would facilitate the work of the table groups, the first task was to analyze the timelines that had already been completed. The reports of the table groups emphasized how St. James' had continually adapted to changes in the larger environment. The congregation had always contributed to the larger society, at times collaborating with other groups. There had always been an emphasis on deepening one's faith through spiritual practices, and programs for learning more about the faith were provided. Although the congregation included many cradle members, there had been a steady stream of new members from other denominations attracted to the liturgy, the more democratic polity of the Episcopal Church, and the community outreach.

At one point during the meeting, the consultants asked the group to form a "fishbowl," with external stakeholders forming a circle in the center of the meeting hall and the congregation sitting around the circle, so they could hear the conversation. The consultant asked the eight or nine people in the circle, "What would happen if St. James' disappeared to-morrow?" The members of the circle, one at a time, described the "tremendous" contribution that the church had made to the community and what a loss its demise would be. They described in detail all the ways members of the congregation gave of their time—to staff the soup kitchen, to manage the hotline for abused women, to help with a teen housing initia-tive, to help with immigration and employment issues, and so forth. At one point the consultant asked the congregation members to raise their hands if they knew about all these ac-tivities. Most of them only knew about two or three of these activities, and they were thrilled to hear about all the ways the congregation was contributing to the community. Each stakeholder was then asked to articulate some of the challenges his or her agency was facing in the coming year. Although at the time St. James' made no commitment to help address these challenges, the church did end up helping with several efforts. One new ministry that came out of the fishbowl was the establishment of an emergency relief fund for people in need of immediate help.

Some of the "sorries" identified by the group were about the failure to address handicapped access and the failure to do more to attract young adults through more diversity in the music and the service. The "prouds" were about continuous community outreach and emphasis on adult formation and spirituality. Participants were also proud of the qualities their two rectors and the assistant pastor brought to the congregation.

The future scenarios were about many of the issues listed above: attracting young adults, incorporating greater diversity in music and liturgy, building handicapped access for both bathrooms and classrooms, and generating new initiatives for mission. But an important by-product of the Future Search conference was the cross-fertilization in the table groups, where those who attended the traditional eight o'clock or ten o'clock services could hear from parents of teenagers about their concerns—the lack of appeal of the worship service, particularly regarding music, for younger people.

## Outcomes

A number of changes and initiatives came out of this event.

- A greater sense of community was evident after the conference, in part because the table groups broke through an eight o'clock/ten o'clock barrier.
- Handicapped access was provided.
- More diverse music was used in worship.
- Established outreach programs were continued, and new ones were initiated.
- Building maintenance issues were addressed.
- St. James' established a Stephen Ministry (lay pastoral visitors).
- The need for services in Spanish was explored.

The warden at the time, when reflecting on the Future Search conference and commenting on outcomes, said he believes the conference influenced what qualities St. James' sought in a new pastor a few years later.

## Our Reflections

The story about Danbury's St. James' Church doesn't start where one would expect. St. James' was in a pretty good place. No big crisis loomed. Membership wasn't tanking, and there weren't any visible financial roadblocks. Members weren't on the edge of civil war about something. The staff seemed stable; no transition was pending. Almost all the other stories we have told are congregations facing urgent issues.

Their real asset was that the church had a group of leaders who were able to see what we call "a hidden crisis." That is, leaders could look beyond the current statistics and members' comfort level and recognize changes in the environment—changes in downtown Danbury, new people moving in, pressure from community needs and people needs. The implications of such changes are large, and wise leaders respond when a crisis, even a hidden one, comes along. This congregation points to an important dimension of leadership: the need to be ahead of the curve.

Every community is probably in the middle of a similar hidden crisis, even when things are fairly peaceful on the surface. In some places, such as urban centers like Danbury, community pressures for change may come more quickly, as demographic change takes place and crime goes up. Congregations in less volatile, perhaps rural, contexts may well have a hidden crisis gathering around them without being fully aware of changes that are occurring. At St. James' leaders saw it coming and decided to head it off. The story shows us that it is not necessary to wait for the crisis to occur, for the transition to surprise us, for the civil war to break out. It is possible to look down the way and prepare for the future of the parish.

Another interesting thing happened at St. James': the leaders' first efforts to do something startled some people. They asked some consultants to help, and the consultants said no. Most people would then do one of two things—talk with another consultant or give up. The leaders decided to engage the consultants more deeply, to push beyond the no. When they did, what developed was a commitment to learn from each other and to engage with one another on a deeper level. The consultants and leaders together formed a planning committee, which turned out to be much more than a planning committee. We think of a planning committee as a group that draws up a plan—a plan that usually gets printed up in a brochure. This committee took responsibility for developing the congregation's life for the future, even to the point of becoming an implementation committee for the Preferred Future that would come out of their effort.

Look at the key activities that went into the development effort. The planning committee defined and recruited all the conference participants—those inside the parish and stakeholders in the community. To help make the small-group discussions more productive, they made sure that each group included people with different perspectives, so that everybody had a chance to hear ideas different from their own. And they designed a way to get special input from outside stakeholders, so they could speak to the congregation from the perspective of their roles in the community.

St. James' Church, like other examples we have given, also found a lot of guidance in its own past story. The use of outside stakeholders brought to the congregation's consciousness parts of the story of which many members were not aware. Interestingly enough for a parish without a visible crisis, the work of this planning group later proved most helpful when the congregation did face a transition in clergy leadership. We might take from this experience a sense of how important the biblical admonition is to "be watchful." It is essential, even while the crises are hidden. Sooner or later, hidden needs for change pop out in transitions or other visible crises. The congregation that simply expects every few years to review its life is likely to discover a payoff when all the hidden issues come to a head sometime in its future.

# A Few Bells and Whistles

We have found that planning teams come up with interesting and creative ideas that make a difference in the large-group meeting. For example, the appreciative banner that First Congregational Church used was an effort all ages could contribute to, one that will likely increase members' sense of belonging. What follows here are some snippets, ideas (1) using World Café to build community and engage the congregation in a conversation around important issues, (2) deepening the priority-setting phase of the conference, and (3) engaging strong value differences in a productive way.

## Becoming a Welcoming Congregation

First Unitarian was a fairly large congregation with two services. The services were just large enough that when attending for the first time, a person could feel lost and lonely. Several members had received feedback from people in the community who had attended one service and then decided to go elsewhere. One of the people who had heard the feedback was familiar with World Café and suggested to board members that they try this approach. The theme would be "How can we become a more welcoming congregation?" and the event would be held on a Saturday, with lunch following. The youth group was invited, and child care was provided. Planners worked hard to make sure that people from both services attended, so they could at least meet. They also made sure that both longtime members and new members attended.

A series of questions introduced each round. The first few rounds were about people's experiences entering a new congregation or new system.

- How did they feel? What were their concerns?
- What did they appreciate? What made a difference?
- What more would they have wished for?
- What do we need to do here?

At the end of each round, people called out summaries of what had been said, and their responses were charted and hung around the room so they were visible. People from both services appreciated the opportunity to meet each other and said they felt that a World Café should be offered more frequently around other issues.

At the end of the last round, specific ideas for becoming more welcoming were suggested. A member of the congregation suggested, "Welcoming is not enough; you have to connect people." As a result the old usher corps (the "hand-out-the-bulletin committee") has been restructured to include new members, new mission, and new ideas. This committee went to a training session specifically to learn more about how to welcome and connect newcomers. The membership has continued to increase. Perhaps the World Café conversation heightened the awareness of the congregation that everyone can do something to welcome others.

## Establishing Priorities for Action

Following an Open Space meeting, notes about a number of initiatives had been placed on the walls for the gathering to prioritize for future action. Everyone was given several adhesive red dots to place on the items they felt strongly about. After they were finished, the pastor had the consultant hand out a green dot, "the God dot," to each person. The pastor asked people to take a few minutes and reflect on where they thought God would have them place the green dot. This exercise shifted the congregation's priorities and resulted in strengthened adult education and active mission.

## Engaging Controversial Issues in Congregations

The following is a format three United Church of Christ congregations used to work with values differences on the theme of becoming "Opening and Affirming." The process is being used in other congregations where there are strongly held differences of opinion. The process does not mean that people change their minds, but it helps people understand a value difference. It helps people maintain relationships with those who have different perspectives.

As in most of the Large Group Methods, people are seated in groups of five or six at round tables. These groups should have a mix of people who have diverse views on the issues to be discussed. Because it is important to make sure people who share the same views are not at the same table, seating must be preassigned. The purpose of the meeting is to bring out and help participants understand as many perspectives as possible about the issue—not to get agreement, reach resolution, or make a decision. This purpose has to be clearly understood at the start.

The person leading the group gives the first question. Each person has a few seconds to write down his or her response to the question. In round-robin style, everyone at each table gives a response. There is no discussion; tablemates just listen to each person's response. When the time indicated below, or a little more, is reached, the leader moves on to the next question.

1. What is your perspective on the issue coming into this conversation? *(two minutes per person)*
2. What life experience do you have that has shaped your perspective on this issue? *(three minutes per person)*
3. What is at the heart of this matter for you? *(two minutes per person)*

4. What is your greatest fear/concern if the position op-
   posite your own wins the day? What is the worst that
   could happen? *(three minutes per person)*
5. Where is there ambiguity about your own perspective?
   What doubts do you have about your own perspective?
   What's your gray area? *(two minutes per person)*
6. What questions of clarification do you have of someone
   else at your table? *(three minutes per person)*
7. What was this process like for you? What have you
   learned? *(Each person gives a brief response to the
   large group.)*

## Conclusions

In all these stories, the need for a change or the need to do an
assessment is identified. The merger of the two synagogues is
an example worthy of reflection, and the following stages are
implicit in all the stories:

- Awareness of the issues (internal and external).
- Ownership of these issues by all.
- Willingness to create a plan of action and to seek a
  better future.
- Willingness *to let go of the known*, and all it
  represented.
- Courage to take the risk and to seek a better future.

St. Peter's, Ocean City, is an especially good detailed study
of the change process. The story describes the steps that were
necessary to get things moving and the activities that are still
going on. The important issue is to nurture and align the
whole church organization—committee structures, services,

reporting relationships, leadership, and internal and external communications—to support the new direction.

Bringing about change in a congregation is not merely a matter of carrying out the steps of a tested process that has been used with success in other settings. Change also requires the ownership of the people *who are the congregation.* Churches and synagogues are voluntary organizations with a few paid staff members, and they depend on members for support. A challenge congregations face today, however, is that with the exception of the few volunteers who have meaningful leadership responsibilities, many of the people who sit in the pews have little sense of membership and involvement. They come because they like the music, the sermons are good, and the church school or religious education is adequate. They come as spectators to a performance, and if it isn't up to their standards, they critique or leave, and maybe go elsewhere. It's a "buyer's market." But "participation," social psychologist Kurt Lewin used to say, "generates commitment." The stories we have told in this section are about *meaningful* involvement. The young man at the Society Hill Synagogue who commented that the Future Search meeting was the first time anyone had ever asked for his opinion made an important point. During the Future Search meeting he had an opportunity to give voice to his opinions on issues that mattered for the future of the synagogue. How do we meaningfully engage the smart and talented people sitting in the pews to help revitalize our congregations?

# Chapter 5
# Stories from Religious Institutions

In THIS CHAPTER, WE RELATE THREE STORIES ABOUT RELIGIOUS institutions—Virginia Theological Seminary in Alexandria, Virginia; the Society of the Sacred Heart, a Roman Catholic religious order headquartered in St. Louis, Missouri; and the Presbytery of Sacramento, California. The first two stories are more complex and reflect major institutional change. The implementation has been carried out over several years, and both institutions are still working on ideas that came out of the original vision for the future and various proposals for organizational change. The third story, which describes how a potentially controversial situation was handled by the presbytery and its members, may be a model for working with similar disagreements.

## Virginia Theological Seminary

Like most seminaries, Virginia Theological Seminary (VTS) had many officially constituted parts, many with quite distinct boundaries: a board of trustees; a faculty including tenured, non-tenured, and adjunct teachers; a student body; a legal relationship to church bodies outside the seminary itself; a body of alumni; and a significant group of benefactors. The seminary bookstore has many customers around the country. There is a continuing-education wing with many participants and alumni, a school for lay theology, and a center for religious education. The change process included a complex coalition of groups, each with its own center of gravity and its own sense of its boundaries.

## Background

Virginia Theological Seminary, the largest of the eleven accredited seminaries of the Episcopal Church, was founded in 1823. The school prepares men and women for lay or ordained leadership and service in the ministry of the church. In its origins it was very much a part of its southern, Episcopal, "low-church" culture. It has close links with the rural southern world in which it began its life.

In the half-century or so following the Second World War, Alexandria and the seminary experienced all sorts of revolutions. Built to accommodate single men and recent college graduates, it began facing a flood of war veterans and a growing constituency of married students. In that postwar era the rural area around Alexandria became a multiethnic urban area, and the previously all-white student body began to integrate. Beginning in the late 1950s the average age of the student body rose as more second-career students entered training. The Episcopal Church's decision in 1976 to open the ordained ministry to women led to further significant change in the student body.

The seminary experienced all the turbulence of twentieth-century America with a changing population not only in the community around it but also in the congregations served by students. The board, the students, and the faculty and administration adjusted and changed to face these challenges, but it was not easy. Each of the groups that were part of the seminary saw the changes from its own perspective, and each constituency had its own preferred pace for dealing with change. By the mid-1990s, however, the board, under its chairman, Bishop Peter Lee of Virginia, and the seminary's dean and president, the Rev. Martha Horne, were in agreement that new strategic planning had to begin.

## Strategic Planning: Future Search Method

During the summer of 1996 the board of trustees authorized the beginning of the planning process and the securing of consultative assistance. Key members of the board, Ed Hall and Lee Camp, became co-chairs of the strategic planning committee, which included members of the board, faculty, alumni, administration, and students. This committee began meeting in early 1997. Board chair Bishop Lee and President and Dean Horne were close to the project and the thinking from the beginning.

The Rev. Vance Johnson (a graduate of another seminary) and Mary Johnson, both of the Institute for Organizational Research and Development, a consulting firm with experience in strategic planning in for-profit and not-for-profit institutions, were chosen as consultants.

The Strategic Planning Committee, with the guidance of the consultants, conducted extensive interviews and listening sessions throughout 1997 with faculty, students, board members, alumni, community leaders, leaders in theological education, and constituent clergy and bishops. This information-gathering yielded multiple ideas and visions for the future of the seminary and indicated that the Future Search process could be fruitful in bringing focus to the various visions. Vance and Mary had experience in this technology, and they and the dean and planning committee agreed to use a form of Future Search for the central planning meeting.

## The Future Search Conference

Early in January 1998, sixty-eight people gathered at a conference center some fifty miles from the seminary. Their task, led by the consultants, was to carry forward strategic planning for the work for the seminary. The participants in the weekend represented a variety of stakeholders in what the seminary was and might need to be in the future. They had been carefully selected and recruited by the Strategic Planning Committee to bring into the same room perspectives not only from the constituencies within the seminary itself, but also from across the church—including thirty dioceses and two countries outside the United States. They represented bishops, priests, and deacons of the church and a wide group of lay leaders. Faculty members and board members, as well as some faculty from other seminaries, were present. Some VTS students were included. Church executives and church leaders of all sorts participated, including some from partner groups outside the Episcopal Church. The planning committee's effective work selecting participants and actively recruiting and organizing them was a key to the positive results of the process.

It should be noted that in keeping with the values and identity of the seminary, the conference was carried out from beginning to end within a framework of a strong worship schedule as an inclusive community that valued the contributions of all conference participants.

The first step in the conference was a scan of the environment of the seminary over the previous few decades. Key events in the lives of the conference participants, in the life of the seminary, and in the external world were gathered on newsprint. Heterogeneous groups of participants analyzed the data to identify the themes or patterns they felt had implications for planning the future of the seminary. Five areas emerged from those discussions:

- Increasing globalization
- Changing roles of laity
- Changing concept of leader
- Erosion of faith and Christian influence in public institutions
- A sense of increasing fragmentation and chaos in the world and the culture

This list was kept on display as a timeline wall for the full conference to ground further discussions.

Small groups of specific stakeholders were then formed to analyze the trends they felt most affected their particular concerns. The stakeholder groups were homogeneous groups, including seven to nine people in a single category, such as seminary students, clergy, faculty members, lay leaders, bishops, and others.

Those groups worked on and then posted some two hundred trends felt to be important by at least one constituency group. Each person was given an opportunity to indicate the intensity of his or her concern about specific trends. The resultant mind map became a visual indicator of the complexity of the trends and the wide disparities among stakeholder groups. Students, for example, were concerned that they be given assistance in understanding and dealing with wide disparities in wealth among those they served, while bishops were concerned about the shortage of clergy, and outside partners were concerned about the aging of the denomination and cultural biblical illiteracy.

After a period of intense personal reflection, prayer, and writing, participants worked in subgroups to share their own visions of what the Spirit might be calling the seminary to do or become. In those subgroups the visions were recast from individual to group, and from word-pictures into creative presentations of what Virginia Seminary might be in 2010.

Each presentation was analyzed and reflected upon—as well as enjoyed!

The final movement of the conference was to discover common ground. First, the entire conference agreed on the key themes for the future, identifying thirteen of them. Those themes were set aside for additional testing, revision, and refinement as a statement of the common ground that the conference had identified and agreed to.

Then the conference again split into smaller groups—each one focusing on one of the Common Ground themes to develop action ideas that might be implemented by the seminary. Some 80 percent of the conference participants agreed to participate in further work on those action ideas. Out of these conversations, the conference developed six objectives:

1. Strengthen residential theological education
2. Enhance development of leaders for the church
3. Expand international initiatives
4. Develop a theological framework for leadership in the church as it moves into the twenty-first century
5. Broaden and strengthen VTS partnerships with other groups engaged in theological education
6. Identify and develop capabilities and resources for the seminary

## Implementation of the Strategic Plan Objective

The seminary board and its committees tested and worked with the six objectives that had been defined by the Future Search conference. Ten months after the conference the board adopted a specific plan based on those six objectives. The board also approved a plan for further implementation and the appointment of two new committees—one to oversee the implementation of the strategic plan, the second to establish priorities for future capital improvements to accomplish the objectives of the strategic plan. The decision to appoint those committees and the work of the committees was key to the implementation of the recommendations, because they provided a location where responsibility rested and where those who needed to implement them could carry out the actions. This step put the objectives into the operating policy of the seminary. Those committees changed the seminary's budget process to make explicit how regular annual budgets served the strategic plan. Future capital improvements were similarly tied to the objectives developed at the Future Search conference.

During the implementation phase that came out of the conference, one important initiative taken by the president and board was the creation of a new seminary position, vice president for institutional advancement. Through that office the seminary institutionalized its commitment to continuing strategic planning. Through these decisions, the board and its chair confirmed continuing commitment to the objectives of the Future Search and to a continuation of strategic planning.

Currently, some time after that conference, each annual operating budget is developed against a template of recommendations from the original planning process. Each year budget allocations are attached to strategic planning objectives. The seminary is now developing plans for capital investment in buildings, repairs, and other efforts; but all such plans are being made in the light of strategic plans made during the planning process.

## Our Reflections

Several things seem important in this story—partly because of the complexity of including sixty-eight diverse stakeholders in one meeting.

- A wide variety of stakeholders from inside and outside the seminary recognized that change was needed.

- The conference input led the board to put a strategy in place to help the seminary move into the future.
- External stakeholders added expertise and perspective.
- The active leadership of the president and the chair of the board was essential—first, in getting the idea accepted and authorized (to say nothing of the funding!); second, in seeing that the findings were fed into the appropriate groups in the seminary so that they could be acted upon.
- The role of the consultants was essential to establishing the overall strategic planning process and the central role of the Future Search conference in that process. Their leadership of the conference included managing the flow of information and integrating the various stakeholders, so that a variety of ideas were considered. The use of the mind map to display data on the walls of the meeting room was an all-important element set up and managed by the consulting team. This visible map of information gave everyone a chance to see the complexity of the organization as the group developed plans for the future.
- The availability of institutional staff members to back up the meeting was invaluable. They helped in the recruiting process and took care of the many arrangements that needed to be attended to for a meeting with many out-of-town participants. A completely volunteer group would have been stretched to carry out such a meeting.

In this case, a strong institution chose to take a hard look at its role and to pay attention to the internal and external perceptions about its role and work. It began to make changes in its operations to respond to what it learned. It gained experience in critical operational skills—paying attention to stakeholders and making organizational adaptations to what was going on in its environment. As a result, VTS is an even stronger institution with a vision shared by stakeholders that has been implemented systematically over the course of several years.

# The Society of the Sacred Heart

This is the story of a Roman Catholic religious community, the United States Province of the Society of the Sacred Heart (SSH-US), and how it faced enormous challenges around its future (see *www.rscjinternational.org* for further information). The journey began in 2002, and the implementation is still going on more than half a decade later. We believe that some of the methods the community used have relevance for judicatories in particular, or for any religious institution that is widely dispersed and would have difficulty bringing people to a central location frequently for a face-to-face meeting. This is also an example of the ingenuity of the planning group and how it succeeded in engaging hundreds of people in planning for the future of the institution. Internet technology, including e-mail as well as teleconferencing, was invaluable. Because of the geographical spread, the teleconferencing calls were timed at 5:00 p.m. eastern time, 4:00 p.m. central time, and 2:00 p.m. Pacific time. Members were able to gather in facilitated regional groups and to participate via speakerphone in group discussions, sharing the information they had collected from interviews and raising questions. Teleconferencing also served as a means for training facilitators, giving them the skills they would need to assist in future work. Melanie A. Guste, RSCJ, wrote the following story.

## How It Started

In the fall of 2002, the Society of the Sacred Heart, United States Province (SSH-US), launched a nationwide planning process with the purpose of dreaming, designing, and planning for the future of the religious community. An eighteen-member planning committee was appointed to develop a long-range planning process. At the same time, the society engaged an actuary to make a report on the financial condition of the institution.

## Background

The U.S. Province of the Society of the Sacred Heart is a community of 462 women located in nineteen geographical areas across the United States. Founded in 1800 in France, the society is today an international community of approximately 3,500 members living in forty-five nations. In 1818 a small group of French women established the community in the United States; its U.S. headquarters is located in St. Louis, Missouri. The society developed a number of schools for girls, both boarding and nonresidential, across the United States. These schools provided a strong liberal arts education for young women. Today they have grown to a network association of twenty-one schools, including both single-sex and coeducational institutions.

The 207 working members of the province are engaged in a wide variety of professional activities and services. Some work in school administration, teaching, pastoral care, nursing, and spiritual direction. Many members today, however, do not work in faith-based settings but are employed as immigration attorneys, psychiatric social workers, college professors, art and music therapists, and executive directors of nonprofit organizations. They all commit to the shared mission statement and to living according to the mission and spirit of the society.

## The Challenges

Listed here are some of the challenges that the organization was facing. These challenges indicated a need for change, for new ideas, structures, and approaches that would help the society move into the future.

### Financial Issues
- Decreasing number of members.
- Low entry rate of new vocations.
- *Rising Healthcare Costs*: Members are living longer, and more members are coming into the later stages of their lives. As the membership reaches a peak in the number of aging members, medical costs rise. Currently the society is operating two quasi-hospitals to accommodate the needs of the elderly retired.
- *Fluctuation in investment income*: This factor has seriously influenced the financial resource picture.

### Geographic Spread
Members are currently living in nineteen geographic areas across the United States, primarily in house "communities." The distance between members consistently poses quality-of-life concerns. As the numbers decrease, this reality has significant financial implications for resource allocation.

### Need for Service
There is no indication that the need for services provided by SSH-US has decreased.

## Other Organizational Issues

- *Hierarchical and bureaucratic modes of leadership*: Top-down methods of organizational functioning are part of the history of the congregation. These methods are used much less now than previously, but they are a concern to many members.
- *Increased desire for participation in decision making*: There has been a defined shift over the years toward an increased sense of ownership for decision making.
- *Outdated vocabulary*: Much of the vocabulary of the SSH describes a way of being more consistent with medieval times than with life in the twenty-first century. While in-house language supports a strong sense of the "corps," it acts as a barrier to others who do not have the dictionary! It does not assist the members to share easily the style of life with others in a user-friendly manner.

## Growing Interest in Regional Gatherings

Over the past ten years, members have been self-organizing into larger and different groupings, some at the regional level. Yet the current government plan still describes the basic units of government as the "house community" and "area." There is a disconnect between what is happening within the system and its governing documents.

# My Role as Change Agent

My role in this case study is, first, as a member of the SSH and, second, as the chair of the planning committee. By profession, I work as an organization/education consultant, facilitator, and mediator. I saw myself functioning within this system as a change agent, as well as working in collaboration with many others.

## The Stakeholders

The main people involved in this case are the 462 members, the primary stakeholders of the mission and organization. There are many secondary stakeholders, including the member schools of the Network of SSH Schools, the 51,000 members of the Associated Alumnae of Sacred Heart Schools (45 member associations), colleagues in sponsored organizations (institutions and organizations that are owned or supported by the SSH), benefactors, and others.

## The Methods Selected

The planning committee selected the Appreciative Inquiry (AI) methodology to begin the planning process. AI involves a systematic way of discovering what gives "life" to a system when it is most alive, effective, and constructively capable in economic, ecological, and human terms. AI involves a way of asking questions that strengthen a system's capacity to heighten the positive potential in an organization. Instead of taking a fix-it approach, the society built on its positive core of two hundred years of practice to identify directions for the future. As the project continued, other methods were used to address the planning issues.

The name we gave to the SSH-US process was "3-D: Dream, Design, and Decide." It was an adaptation of "The Four-D Appreciative Inquiry Summit Meeting" (described in chapter 3). In the SSH-US model the discovery phase was merged into the dream phase. What follows is a description of what occurred in each phase.

### Phase 1: Dream
*Step 1*: The process was launched with a video, "Celebrate What's Right with the World" by DeWitt Jones (Jones, 2001). This video was distributed to the nineteen geographic areas

in advance of the national teleconference. Appropriate to the Appreciative Inquiry approach, this video focuses on the power of vision to create new positive images for transformation. It was followed by a teleconferencing discussion.

*Step* 2: This step was a series of face-to-face interviews. In advance of these interviews the planning committee designed and distributed an interview protocol to be used as a guide throughout the society. In addition to providing the protocol, members of the committee trained nineteen local facilitators in the AI interview process via a national conference call. After receiving the training, members in nineteen geographical areas interviewed one another. Following the interviews between members, stakeholder interviews were held. The planning committee modified slightly the interview protocol for use with the secondary stakeholder groups. Here are some of the questions asked in the stakeholder and member interviews:

- Describe in detail the best experiences you have had with the society.
- Describe a time when you felt your perspective and presence contributed to the society.
- What is the *core* value of the Society of the Sacred Heart?
- What three wishes do you have for the Society in the United States?

After the interviews the interviewers filled out a form recording what was memorable about the interview, what two or three themes stood out the most during the interview, and what the person interviewed wished for the society.

*Step* 3: Data from all of the interviews were collected, compiled, and distributed by the planning committee via a Web-based "Report on Key Themes and Wishes." This electronic report illuminated those themes that emerged from across the country, allowing members across the large geographic spread of the United States to compare systemwide themes and wishes with those identified within each geographic area. Five key systemwide themes emerged from the interview process: (1) government and leadership; (2) spirituality; (3) education mission, ministry, and programs; (4) membership and community; and (5) finances and resources. Discussions were launched on the Web site so that members could discuss these themes.

## A Critical Turn

The actuary who had been hired to provide comprehensive information on organizational finances and demographics submitted her report, which was not designed as a part of the 3-D process but affected its direction. The report presented information that was difficult and new to many in the society. It was distributed across the system as one indicator of the current situation and was intended to open up new possibilities for action. A national teleconference call was held so that members could begin a formal conversation about current mind-sets, assumptions, and realities. Following this teleconference, two types of feedback loops were designed: (1) a Web-based discussion whereby members could continue to dialogue about the current reality, and (2) an e-mail exchange between the members and the leadership team, to enable members to ask questions about the actuarial data that might be of a more personal nature.

Although the data from the actuarial report were not new, the arrival of the report was a difficult moment in the planning process. The actuarial data created a new level of awareness. As one member put it, "This was a wake-up call." The information could no longer be ignored or postponed. It posed significant financial dilemmas for the organization. At the same time the Appreciative Inquiry process had injected hope into the system and had helped stakeholders recognize the foundational core values of the institution. A new resilience emerged in response to the actuarial report. A group of 30 members was convened in St. Louis to reflect on members' comments about the actuarial data and to identify additional data and resources needed for planning. Another national teleconference was held at the end of this meeting, during which members had an opportunity to ask questions of the actuary. The outcome of this process was the formation of eight actuarial study groups consisting of members as well as other experts to serve as resources. Actuarial follow-up studies included (1) health-care costs and retirement options, (2) pension options, (3) prescription-drug programs, (4) real estate, (5) salaries, benefits, and self-employment, (6) comparative costs of living singly vs. living in community, (7) society-sponsored projects, and (8) contributions to anti-poverty ministries.

To wrap up the first year, the thirteen chairpersons of the society's standing committees who work on matters related to the religious life met to strengthen existing linkages within the society. This was the first meeting of its kind in the history of the SSH-US Province. An outcome from this meeting was an interactive Web-based calendar to foster greater connections across the system. A lively Web report, complete with photos, news reports and other data, testimonies, and summaries, was used to communicate to the membership.

In preparation for the design phase, presentations were made about Appreciative Inquiry and the 3-D process at the national conferences of the Network of Sacred Heart Schools and at meetings with Associates of the SSH.

## Phase 2: Design
The design phase began with an extensive application of Rosemary Luling Haughton's *Images for Change: The Transformation of Society* (Mahwah, N.J.: Paulist Press, 1997). This

approach uses the metaphor of a house to probe and reimagine the structures of social institutions and organizations. The purpose of the method introduced here was to generate ideas about how to improve the design of the system and continue the plan for the future. Meetings were held in the nineteen geographic areas, and data from across the system were collected to develop an insightful and lively picture of "the SSH-US as a house." Here are some sample questions:

- How would you describe this house in terms of its size? Is the house the right size for us now?
- Who is responsible for this house?
- What do the owners of the house do?
- Are there of signs of aging or deterioration of the house—cracks in the walls, leaks in the roof?
- What about the windows that let in the light? What opportunities do we see?

A comprehensive report was developed from the data collected and, once compiled, it was disseminated to all participants via a national teleconference. In the last movement of this phase of the process, stakeholders met in groups of five or more in regional, area, multi-area, or self-selected groups to envision the future. After the possibility statements were developed, members and stakeholders, using all of the data from previous sessions, developed proposals around the core issues of the SSH-US. A guide was developed that included questions to consider in developing proposal statements. These were customized according to the presenting issues of the society. Two questions were developed to guide these groups:

1. When you think about the best experiences of the past and the most compelling calls of the present, how would you produce an organizational chart,

design a flowchart, or construct a model that depicts your vision for the future?

2. When you recall the best experience of our shared history and the most compelling calls of the present, what images or metaphors come to your mind and heart that expresses the emergent future of the SSH-US?

Responses were forwarded to representatives of the planning committee, who compiled the statements into a printed and Web-based report.

The five key themes previously mentioned emerged consistently: (1) government and leadership; (2) spirituality; (3) education mission, ministry, and programs; (4) membership and community; and (5) finances and resources. Related sub-issues were added. The chart on the following page shows the emergent key themes to related subtopics.

Five improvement teams (IT) were formed to develop more specific proposals around the topics and related sub-issues. These member-driven improvement teams were important. Members were encouraged to serve on teams as researchers, writers, secretaries, and the like. The team members identified team coordinators. Improvement team communication meetings were held through teleconferences. A planning committee member served on each IT as a "tracker." Improvement team electronic forums were opened on the Web for sharing work on proposals. Face-to-face meetings of the improvement teams were scheduled in four cities to synthesize the crafted proposals and to develop additional proposals. A guide called "Outline for a Constructive Proposal" was developed to standardize the writing format and the output of proposals. All of the resources developed during previous stages of the process were made available to the teams' synthesis-writing groups for the development of proposals.

| GOVERNMENT AND LEADERSHIP | SPIRITUALITY | EDUCATIONAL MISSION, MINISTRY, AND PROGRAMS | MEMBERSHIP AND COMMUNITY | FINANCES AND RESOURCES |
|---|---|---|---|---|
| Decision making | Relationship with Roman Catholic Church | Sponsored programs (CEDC, FARM, etc.) | Health care | Real estate |
| Leadership (model and process) | Lifestyle (where and how we live) | Relationship with the Network | Living singly | Investments |
| Roles and responsibilities of Provincial Team. Area directors, members, etc. | Differing theologies and worldviews | Visibility in community—corporate identity | Wellness—physical and mental well-being and health | TIAA/CREF and other pension options |
| Assemblies | Fostering Cor Unum | Relationship with AASH | Diversity | Insurance—medical, car |
| Organizational structure and style (area, matrix, visual, etc.) | Articulation of our spirituality for today | Goals for mission and ministry | Local community | Contributions to poverty ministries: Phillipine Fund and Fund for Ministry |
| Organizational process—decision making | Reconciliation and forgiveness | Relationship with international community | Area community | Rent vs. purchase |
| Internal communications, including technology | Prayer and spirituality with others | External communication, including technology | Retirement age/options | Loans |
| Leadership development | Strengthening contemplative spirit | Relationship with associates | Promoting vocations to the Society | Prescription programs |
| Formation (membership and structure) | | Volunteer program | Assimilation in USA culture (consumerism, individualism, etc.) | Salaries, benefits, and self-employment |
| Technology | | Development | | Administrative costs |
| | | | | Budget development |

As a result of the work of the members, stakeholders, and improvement teams, sixty-five proposals were developed for the consideration of the members. These were posted on the Web site for all members to review. The development of these proposals signaled the end of the design phase, and the beginning of the "decide phase" of the 3-D process.

## Phase 3: Decide

The "decide phase" of the process consisted of three major activities:

- Web-based survey of feedback on proposals.
- Meetings in areas for a straw poll.
- Regional summit meetings (open assemblies) of the whole membership for dialogue and formal decision on proposals.

The regional assemblies were the culmination of the decide phase. All members of the SSH-US were invited to participate in one of four assemblies. Twice each day, the entire membership was linked via national teleconference to hear reports from different groups about discussions and presentations on specific proposals under consideration, and to ask clarifying questions. Through the teleconferencing, members could hear the system-wide results of votes taken on proposals. Results of local voting were called into a central person, who compiled the results. Twenty-nine proposals were passed. The gatherings were times of celebrating the decisions of the members about the future of the SSH-US. After the assemblies members were given an opportunity to evaluate the whole process. The proposals were forwarded to an assembly implementation group for follow-up.

## Outcomes from Part 1

What follows is the feedback from the evaluations, combined with the reflections of the planning committee members:

- As a result of the collaborative effort, the SSH-US made decision on sixty-five proposals regarding the future of the organization.
- The planning process culminated in the creation of an assembly implementation committee that will develop an action plan to manage the proposals agreed on by the members.
- The process increased the sense of inclusion of the members.
- Certain tools and techniques were introduced into the organization for participatory decision making—electronic surveys, straw polls, consensus, and voting.
- The organization moved forward with regard to the integration of technology into its daily life. Members learned to use the Web to strengthen community, and they became familiar with many of the features of online processes.
- New leadership emerged as many members took part as facilitators, team leaders, study coordinators, committee members, and the like. Many members received training in facilitation skills.
- The organization discovered the widespread need for updating its hardware and software, and for retraining its members. The organization committed to on-going financial support of technology within the community.

- Through the regular use of teleconferences, the organization learned how to bring the system together across geographical space and to engage in substantive discussions.
- The planning process facilitated the identification of the types of leadership, skills, and style needed at this time for the organization.

## Implementation

The provincial, Kathleen Hughes, asked Jean Bartunek, RSCJ, to head the assembly implementation committee. Bartunek is professor of organizational studies at Boston College and a past president of the Academy of Management. As you read through this section, note the chart that was used for tracking each proposal (see page 105). Across the top of the chart were the following headings: proposal number, the purpose of the proposal, who is in charge of the implementation, and the status of the implementation to date. What follows is Bartunek's story of the work of this committee.

### The Background

When each proposal was posted on the Web site, one or more persons were also posted as the primary sponsors. What I initially assumed was that the sponsors had been very instrumental in crafting the proposals, and so I thought that my committee should include someone from each proposal that was passed. However, I learned from the provincial team that the list of sponsors didn't signify who had actually worked on the proposals. So we formed a committee that included representatives who had worked on each of the five topic areas.

### The Challenges

One of the first issues that had to be addressed was the work of this committee. Some province members expected our com-

| Current Proposal # | Original IT Group Proposal # | Proposal Name and Purpose | Who's in Charge of Implementation? | Status of Implementation to This Point |
|---|---|---|---|---|
| 4 | G9 & E10 | Proposal for technology education and resources for the US province: This proposal is intended to ensure competence, co-learning, and greater ease of communication in order to strengthen the bonds of the membership in cost-effective and knowledge-sharing ways. | Technology Committee | The Technology Committee has added new members. Paula Toner is the Provincial Team Liaison. |
| 7 | F3 | Criteria for Initiating New Society Projects: The purpose of this proposal is to develop criteria for initiating and stating new efforts. | Provincial Team | A process with specific criteria was articulated in the 2001 version of a document called Process for Ministry Change. This was distributed to the province in 2001 and is already posted on the Web under the Policies and Guidelines section of the RSCJ Only Website. |
| 14 | A | Articulating our spirituality through research and writing: We propose that a team be designated to coordinate the process of articulating our spirituality through research and writing in order to share this essential value of our lives with new understanding and greater availability. | Fran Gimber, Mary Frohlich | Mary Frohlich and Fran Gimber are champions for this proposal. With Mary Blish, Barbara Bowe, Sharon Karam, Lyn Osiek, and Barbara Quinn, they are developing three initiatives: (1) a website where articles published in the past (e.g., in RSCJ Journal or other sources), as well as new essays, can be posted; (2) a group to translate and interpret selected historical sources; and (3) a consultation on a possible book project. More information on these will be provided on the teleconference. |

mittee to implement the proposals, but I didn't think this was a good plan. I reached an agreement with the provincial team when I was chosen as chair and before the other members were recruited that clarified our boundaries, particularly that we were not doing the implementing ourselves, though we would coordinate with and assist implementers.

Another challenge we faced was that far too many proposals had been passed (twenty-nine of the original sixty-five) for us to work with, and some of these were overlapping. A third challenge was that some of those who had sponsored proposals had done so only because someone had asked them to, but they had little or no interest in developing them further. A related issue was that some people had written proposals only as a communication device (for example, they wanted to tell people how to take care of some society-owned property). They also had no interest in developing the proposals further. Finally, a large number of proposals about "government" had been submitted to the assembly. Almost none of these had passed, but several members really wanted something done about the issues regardless. We had to be clear that our mandate was to deal only with proposals that had passed.

## How the Challenges Were Managed

We established a clear boundary about what our work as a committee entailed. We were not the implementers, but we were there to support, encourage, and coordinate those responsible for implementation of those proposals that had passed the assembly.

We worked hard to make sense of the proposals, to combine them when appropriate, and to identify the proposals for which there was energy. In some other cases we worked hard to engage province members in sponsoring implementation of proposals, and some of our efforts worked better than others.

Some of the province administrative "offices" had laid out as proposals the work they needed to do anyway. For such proposals we simply communicated with the offices on the work they were already doing and encouraged them to communicate with the province members.

## The Work of the Committee

We organized the proposals requiring implementation by creating a chart, which indicated the name of the proposal, its purpose, who or what group was the sponsor or implementer, and the status to date of the proposal's implementation. Each of us on the committee served as contact person for some of the proposals. We kept in close touch with the implementers and tried to encourage them. We also communicated regularly with the province in writing and in teleconferences on their implementation of proposals.

## Outcomes

A good number of initiatives have been implemented.

*Health care for the elderly*: Our province had been running nursing homes without benefit of Medicare, and this reponsibility was a huge financial drain. A group that was already working on this topic had submitted a proposal for dealing with this issue. The group members did an excellent job on this complex and difficult topic, and we supported them as well as we could. Since early 2006, because of their efforts, elderly religious in need of serious care are moving to Medicare-sponsored facilities.

*Financial issues*: A large number of proposals had to do with finance. There have been several positive changes in finance based on implementation of the proposals. In particular, a mission advancement office has been functioning very effectively.

*Higher education*: As a result of the work of our committee, a meeting was scheduled at the University of San Diego for those involved in higher education in our order. In preparation for this meeting a small group put together a statement of goals and criteria for SSH-US involvement in higher education.

*Spirituality*: A spirituality subcommittee has taken initiative and has been active on a number of fronts. For example, the group sponsored an extraordinary provincewide teleconference in which four members of the province spoke movingly on "how I see myself living our spirituality today."

*Annual reports*: It used to be that just the provincial team wrote an annual report to the province. Now each committee writes such a report as well, and this practice helps to make evident how many members of the province are involved in its work.

*The decision-making process*: We began to provide ongoing communication in the province about the implementation of the proposals. In addition, we supported initiatives on some items that would otherwise not have been pursued. We were careful to stay out of the decision-making process for the individual proposals, other than strongly encouraging province members to implement them.

## Ongoing Work

Many of the proposals were still being implemented five years after this effort began. Eldercare is still an issue, though a large number of strides have been taken. Changes are still in process in the finance office. Mission advancement will be an important office in our province for years. The spirituality subcommittee is still taking initiatives. The higher education meeting was being planned.

Overall, I think our committee did a good job. We didn't take over for others, but we did encourage them as well as we could. In some instances we helped something happen, although in other instances, when it was clear that there was no energy for implementation, we let the proposal drop. We also supported some initiatives that might have been developed anyway, but we kept them in the forefront of the province's attention.

## Our Reflections

We have a remarkable piece of learning available to us as we reflect on the planning process in an admittedly complex organization.

There are exciting things to learn here—how wise management can accomplish unexpected outcomes by carefully setting in place new work groups, using new communications techniques, and arranging complex interactions between groups that do not ordinarily meet. The list is impressive. What developed is a textbook for others who want to approach change in a diverse, geographically separated constituency. Even groups that are not as large or as geographically challenged can find clues about how adapting methods and technology can be situational. That is, that by making wise adaptations rather than using routine methods, one may be able to crack open almost any change opportunity and work for deeper dimensions of the needed change.

That's a first-level reflection on this remarkable story. Perhaps the easiest lesson to learn is this: what these people did in a complex situation can be transferred to other complex situations, but also SSH-US provides clues to those who want to change even simpler systems.

There are other issues to reflect upon:

1. The work of the planning committee was ingenious. We note this because what was done looks so simple. ("Everybody has a planning committee. What's so important about this one?") But it was not simple. The planning committee

was called into being in a system that did not have linkages that reflected the current state of the organization and its environment. Many parts of the organization were not in clear connection with others. Communications were a problem. Even governance was unsettled. The planning committee had to make decisions in a dispersed organization—decisions that helped the entire organization address multiple issues, learn to set priorities, and begin to implement directions.

2. The planning committee created an operating communication system to replace a hierarchical communication system that had been developed for an earlier time. The new communication system used some technology and some new ways for groups to form and work together, so that a new way of working on common issues became the norm.

3. The implementation committee made some important critical decisions: the committee's work was to be limited. It was to focus on "managing proposals toward implementation," not "implementation" per se. Its primary task had to do with establishing a method for follow-up, not with producing particular products or programs.

4. The implementation team helped establish a way for the whole organization to understand the priority-setting process and to take appropriate responsibility for implementation and reporting. This was done through the following:

- Clarifying that if there is no energy or sponsorship around a proposal, no matter how good people think the proposal is, it is dropped from consideration.
- Selecting the important issues and getting them on somebody's agenda or under someone's sponsorship.
- Monitoring the implementation of the twenty-nine proposals by keeping in touch with the province.
- Setting up a system of monthly reports from each group that is implementing proposals.

Many of the important issues for the Society, particularly the financial ones, were or are being addressed. A significant change that happened was a process change, a change in the way important issues were addressed and may be addressed in the future.

# The Presbytery of Sacramento, California

We believe that conflict is a major issue in denominations today. A recent clergy workshop had the title "Bringing about Change without Wreaking Havoc." An issue of *The Economist* carried the theme "Brains, Not Bullets." The question for faith-based communities is not too different—how can we stay together, and work and worship together, when we hold strong differences around important values?

## Background

This is the story of the Presbytery of Sacramento, California, and how it worked with mistrust and differences of opinion around a potentially volatile situation—proposed changes to *The Book of Order*, the basic document by which Presbyterians at all levels guide their denominational life. In the Presbyterian system, every year each presbytery works to come to agreement on important denominational issues, and the presbytery vote then goes to the General Assembly to be tallied with the votes from all the other presbyteries. A recurring problem is that often the "big" issues are *so* big and sometimes so controversial that the argument gets very heated, and angry teams form on all sides. In such a heated situation, people often accuse others of bad faith (or no faith, as the case may be). Words that are needed to clarify issues and sort out alternatives end up becoming weapons that can work real and lasting hurt on people who genuinely love the church and the presbytery. Sacramento had recently experienced strong reactions around similar situations and realized that in 2007 several more issues were coming up that could provoke strong disagreements. Presbytery members had experienced enough debates and arguments that diminished their trust in each other and in their system. They had come to feel they needed new ways to disagree without attacking, to hold fast to important values without denigrating the values of others. Could they disagree without breaking the presbytery's sense of community that meant so much to them?

Two distinct groups are involved in this story—the presbytery council, which leads and make plans for the presbytery, and the presbytery itself, which includes commissioners from all the congregations and the clergy members. The council decided to hold a retreat for the council itself prior to the meeting of the whole presbytery. Below, we first describe the council meeting. In the case of the presbytery meeting, an interesting shift occurred: the council departed from its usual way of operating with one meeting for the presbytery, and planned for two meetings. In their first meeting participants would focus on understanding each other and the issues, developing skills in communicating effectively with one another around important issues. In the second meeting, they would make decisions by voting.

## Challenges Facing the Council and the Presbytery

- Members of the council felt there was a lack of trust between the Sacramento Presbytery Council and the members of the presbytery.
- Several large congregations in the Sacramento Presbytery were unhappy with the direction in which the Presbyterian Church (U.S.A.) was moving.

- Some members of the Sacramento Presbytery questioned the authority of the council to make decisions between meetings of the presbytery.
- The General Assembly of the Presbyterian Church (U.S.A.) asked every presbytery to vote on certain proposed amendments to *The Book of Order*. Many of these amendments could potentially lead to conflict.

## What Happened?

A decision was made by the council to look for a consultant to work first with the Council of Presbytery and later to work with the Sacramento Presbytery. Lisa Beutler, who was selected, brought experience in handling conflict situations and broad knowledge and experience in the field of organizational development. Lisa, who had also worked with congregations before, is the associate director of the Center for Collaborative Policy at California State University, Sacramento. She worked with a core planning committee to design both the council and the presbytery meetings.

## The Presbytery Council Meeting

A decision was made to hold a retreat in December 2006 for the council, approximately thirty members, using many of the activities that occur in a Future Search meeting, as described in chapter 3. Appreciative Inquiry–type questions were also incorporated into the meeting. Council members were seated in small groups that were a microcosm of the presbytery, mixing people at different tables by roles and viewpoints.

The meeting began with a welcome and an opening prayer, followed by a short talk by the consultant on the ground rules for holding "worthy conversations." The council meeting included five phases.

1. *The Church at Its Best.* Each person was asked to share a story from either his or her congregation or the presbytery about a time when the church was at its best. Then each small group selected characteristics the stories demonstrated, and these characteristics were shared by tables in the large group.

2. *Where Have We Been?* Using a timeline exercise, participants examined the pre-1965 period and then the period from 1965 until 2006. Four timelines were used: self (What was happening to you during this period?), the presbytery, the Presbyterian Church, and the United States and the world. Groups then analyzed the timelines for the themes that emerged and looked at how events from one timeline were linked to others. Some interesting insights emerged from the analysis and discussion. During the long history of the Presbyterian Church, there had always been dissension and breakaway congregations. There were also splits in which new denominations were formed.

3. *Where Are We Now?* By tables, participants analyzed trends facing the presbytery today, including demographic shifts, political shifts, economic issues, and so forth. This analysis was followed by small-group discussions about two questions: (1) What is the current presbytery's response to this trend? (2) What would be the preferred response to this trend? The small table groups shared their insights with the large group.

Then there was a break in the discussion for personal prayers. In the small groups, each person articulated something personal for which the group's prayers were desired.

4. *The Council at Its Best ("Prouds" and "Sorries").* The next discussion session focused on four questions:

- When is the council at its best?
- What new strengths does the council need to build?

- What should we carry forward? What should we leave behind?

Again, small groups reported on their conversations to the large group.

5. *Where Are We Going? The Role of the Council in 2007.* Still working in small groups, participants next reflected on the following:

- What do the church and members need from the council?
- How do we define council leadership?
- How do we define success for the council for 2007?

Tables reported to the large group, and then participants adjourned for a business meeting.

## Goals and Commitments for 2007

As a result of the council meeting, a statement of goals and commitments was put together for 2007, the coming year. Some of the goals refer to *internal* council issues: conduct well-planned meetings, revisit council structure, explore alternative forms of decision making, improve council education, connect people, get anchored to the presbytery. Other goals for the year dealt with *external* issues: use presbytery meetings to strengthen congregational values, stay aware of presbytery pulse, practice better and more frequent communication, explore alternative methods of decision making, intentionally draw out voices, foster spiritual nourishment, sponsor presbytery-wide retreat events to build relationships.

## Reflections by Council Members on the Meeting

One of the members summed up the comments participants had made:

I want to echo what others have already said and let you know that I thank God that our presbytery, at this particular time, has this particular group of people sitting around the table at council. I was humbled yesterday again at the way God works when a community of people are gathered together who may or may not see everything the same way but who are committed to doing God's will (whatever that may be), and doing it with love and grace. It was powerfully confirmed for me that any decision that this group faces, no matter how difficult, will be made well as long as we make it together after much listening, honesty, and prayer. I am humbled to be a part of this group and have realized that I stand to learn a great deal from every person around the table.

## The Presbytery at Work

The purpose of this meeting of the Sacramento Presbytery, held in February 2007, was to ensure that the proposed amendments to *The Book of Order* and their implications were fully understood prior to a vote, which was held in May 2007. Results of that vote were sent to the General Assembly of the Presbyterian Church (U.S.A.) to be tallied with the votes from the other presbyteries. There is a lot of wisdom in first making sure that constituents understand the issues before making decisions about them. Lisa Beutler, the consultant, helped facilitate this meeting with the elected representatives of the churches in the presbytery and their presbytery council. Several documents were provided to the participants before the meeting. An amendment booklet was mailed to each of the congregations and was also available online.

### The Agenda
    1. Presentation: Decision-making and Conflict
    2. Presentation: Worthy Conversations

3. Dialogue on Amendments to *The Book of Order*
4. Reports on Dialogue

The goal of this meeting was to gain genuine understanding of the different perspectives, yet maintain relationships. Lisa Beutler, rather than providing mere facilitation, began the meeting with two presentations based on her background in consulting, one about conflict in decision-making situations and the other about how to hold worthy conversations. Here are excerpts from her talk and some of the key points she made:

> Corrosive conflict occurs when one or several parties feel unseen, unheard, or unappreciated. Conflict may occur when one or several of the parties involved behave in a different manner from what the group [members] believe they agreed upon on and what they think should be happening. In some cases these are un-negotiated expectations.
>
> In many situations collaboration, in the best use of it, is a powerful and effective tool to get a win-win outcome. But collaboration is not the right tool for every situation. For example, collaboration is not a good tool when the issues involve basic values or principles. People should not be asked to negotiate their values.

She also challenged the group by asking: "How can people be in conflict yet continue to maintain relationships, and feel seen, heard, and appreciated? How can decisions be better informed? How can people learn from one another without compromising their integrity? How can people be in worthy conversations?"

For the dialogue on amendments to *The Book of Order*, members were seated in small pre-set mixed groups, and each group was asked to review a specific proposed amendment. Each amendment, therefore, would be considered by at least one group. People at the tables were asked individually to write down their responses to the following questions:

- What is this amendment about? Why is it being discussed at this time?
- What works for you? Why?
- What does not work for you? Why?
- What are the surprises or unexpected consequences (good or bad) that might result from the change?
- What questions would you like to have answered before you make a final decision?

The table group, after hearing each individual's responses to the questions, discussed the following:

- What types of themes do you see in the responses?
- If you could change the amendment to make it work for you, what would you change? What are the underlying principles or foundational beliefs that led you to this perspective?
- What did you learn from this conversation?

Each table summarized for the whole group the dialogue on the specific amendment it had studied.

## Members' Reflections on the Process

The following are some of the comments that were made at the end of the meeting; what participants had learned, and what they had come to understand, particularly about how differently each person may view an issue.

"I learned about the importance of really reading and asking questions rather than just jumping to conclusions and making assumptions."

"After listening to people with really divergent views, I recognized that people read things very differently from the way I read them."

"Hearing the differences helped me understand how some of the past misunderstanding had occurred. We should have taken more time to understand different points of view."

"I started to think about ways to address the concerns, rather than arguing about the proposed solution."

## Our Reflections

As we reflected on this story, we discovered that it did not represent primarily a way to make decisions about changing objectives, directions, or programs—as the VTS and Sacred Heart stories did. It was a story of how a large, complex organization might change the climate within which it made decisions, so that its total life would be strengthened. In fact, those other stories did have a healthy impact on how those institutions worked, as well as on what matters they worked on. But in this story the focus is on the process, not the outcomes.

The way this story goes, however, also makes another very important point: a task that doesn't look too big may actually be much larger than it looks. Religious organizations often zip immediately from identifying a problem to making decisions and plans for implementation. People seem to think that is a wise way to operate. In this story, though, the leaders and consultant recognized that their previous decision-making process might not have worked very well. Trust was low; people were dreading the next presbytery meeting and the controversy that might erupt. Leaders made a decision to "make haste slowly." They separated the actions to be taken, so each could be dealt with more effectively. The leadership group was given a chance to walk through the minefields and learn new ways to walk. Then, strengthened by new skills and insight, they split apart the tasks of "understanding" the changes and "voting" on them. This gave them time to explore the issues and how differently various people felt about them. It gave them time to explore without having to decide, to test ideas rather than having immediately to make irrevocable choices, to try to understand positions other than their own, to listen rather then prepare a defense of one's own position or a counterargument to other positions, and to listen—listen to each other and to God.

Slowing down the action made understanding possible. Consensus can come when both sides of a conflict understand and honor the position of the other. What we see in this story approaches the style of discernment—it takes longer, but it tends to lead to more secure and lasting decisions.

Another reflection we have here is the importance of the leadership team's being guided by somebody who has good conflict-transformation skills but is not a party to the debate—the consultant. Her role made it possible for her to do some teaching about how meetings can be more productive, how participants can relate more creatively, and how ordinary people can make way for grace to appear even in mundane organizational life.

# Our Reflections:
# Congregational and Institutional Stories

What do these stories tell us about congregational change and changes in religious institutions?

The desire for change arises from various sources. Sometimes a group within the congregation or organization is concerned that internal and external issues are not being addressed. At other times, environmental pressures—changing demographics, societal changes, technological changes, financial change, increased marketplace competition—bring about change. Often people within these communities of faith dream dreams, see opportunities, and have a vision of future possibilities. Richard Beckhard, well-known professor of management at MIT and one of the founders of the field of Organization Development, used a formula to describe what is needed for change to occur: $D+V+N > R$, dissatisfaction plus vision, plus next steps, he would say, overcomes resistance to change, but all three elements on the left side of the formula need to be present for real change to occur.

People, whether in a congregational setting or a religious institutional setting, have ideas about what needs to be fixed, what needs to be done for the future, what areas need improvement. In an institution the finance people have one view, the professors may have another, the persons responsible for religious education in a congregation have another view, and people involved in outreach have their views. Everyone has a piece. This phenomenon is often described as "silo thinking." People fight for their area, their preferences, and the priorities they see as important. There is strength in this approach, because it provides focus, good ideas, and commitment, and it can produce remarkable results. There is also a handicap in silo thinking: overfocusing on one area can result in our being unaware of what other groups are doing and often discounting their work and putting obstacles in the way.

The approaches described in this book address this problem. The mantra "Get all the people in the room" means to make sure that all the silos are represented when the meeting is held, and that the subject is one that the whole "farm," not just the silo, can identify with. Everyone is on the same hayride. Make sure that participants are in small mixed groups (that is, mix up the silos). We are also expanding the meaning of silos and farm. Continuing with this analogy, we are reminded that we cannot fully determine the future of the farm without

looking at the external environment. We may need someone
from the state agricultural department; we might want to invite
some customers and suppliers, other farmers from the county,
and someone from the agricultural school at the university.
When everyone is in the room, we can focus on the preferred
future. We do not need to defend our own perspective. We can
focus on how each area of interest or concern can contribute
to that desired future and how each can assist the other. The
focus shifts to ensuring the effectiveness of the whole farm in
the context of the larger environment. We can all apply this
metaphor to the religious institutions that matter to us.

In the stories we have told in this book, readers have
learned what Large Group Methods can do.

1. They break down the silos, so the issues of the whole
   institution or congregation come into focus.
2. They release new energy and new ideas that are then
   available for working with systemwide issues.
3. Differences and conflicts lose their power as people
   move into mutual listening, collaborate across the
   boundaries, and build new relationships and new alli-
   ances for the good of the whole.
4. Ownership becomes broader. People who have had less
   opportunity to participate move to the center when they
   are invited to share their insights and experience being
   genuinely listened to. They have more sense of belonging and become more willing to support the preferred
   future and commit to working toward the vision.
5. Outside perspectives and the focus on the external
   environment in which the congregation or institution
   exists give rise to new understandings, insights, and
   opportunities.
6. The vision of what the organization is called to do is
   broadened in two ways. The listening and the sharing

from voices that have not previously been in the conversation enhance and enlarge the basic vision. The new vision becomes the vision of the expanded community, with far more people committing themselves to the community and to the vision.

Working together, we need to expand the vision of our congregations and religious institutions. We need to challenge and inspire the members, enhancing our ability to carry out our calling.

# Chapter 6
# Change Is a Process, Not an Event

WHAT WE HAVE BEEN LEARNING, AND WHAT THE STORIES IN THIS book have demonstrated, is that change is not an event or a program. It is a long-term process that goes through phases, waxes and wanes, but never stops.

We have come to see that it ordinarily has three phases. The three phases of the cycle articulate for us the dynamic nature of what we are trying to do. Each organization has its own unique timetable. Some spend a long time in preparation, then carry out the central task of the "big meeting" with dispatch. And there is much variation in the amount of time groups devote to the time we describe as "endings and new beginnings." Nobody handles the process exactly the same way others do it. We encourage innovation and creative energy from the special people who are part of the process in each place. The stories we told in chapters 4 and 5 show how each group approached the overall cycle and its phases using its own "group personality."

## Stage One: Preparation

Every need for change begins either with a discomfort or an opportunity that is felt strongly by an individual or small group. The organization's formal leader may be the first to become aware that something needs to be addressed. Often the need is felt as a "call" to be or do something better. Often, however, it is not the official leader who senses the need or opportunity. Sometimes it is first felt and acted on by a small group that wants to "reform" something. One of the ordinary committees or task forces of the current structure may hit a snag or see a larger need, beyond its own work.

That person or group is evidence of a prophetic stirring. The task to be addressed at that stage, if real change is to come, is to broaden the concern or vision, to involve others in it, to test whether it truly reflects a call or just pipe dreams or frustration. If others come to believe the possibility that one visionary or group sees is worth working on, the call then must be authorized to be an operative planning function.

At Virginia Theological Seminary (VTS), the need appeared from the top. The board, the chair of the board, and the seminary president recognized a need to take a serious look at the future. But all the constituencies of the seminary—faculty, alumni, the congregations it served, and various agencies of the region—had to be brought on board.

In the United States Province of the Society of the Sacred Heart (SSH-US), apparently many voices from many groups began to raise questions about the status quo that needed to be addressed. These prophetic questions appeared almost simultaneously, and a plethora of proposals (sixty-five of them!) for change collected at headquarters. Some changes were related to operational problems, some to new opportunities that could be grasped.

At St. Peter's United Methodist Church in Ocean City there was a widespread feeling among many, a realization that things were not going well. Threats were building up that had to be addressed. Losses of members and finances added pressure. It was the new pastor who gave voice to that need and articulated it as a new vision of the future.

At "the other" St. Peter, the Missouri Synod Lutheran church, the new stirring came from the middle. After a long pastorate, as the congregation tried to figure out how to prepare for a new pastor, as our story put it, "a small group began tinkering with new projects."

In each case, a planning group was formed and began by defining the tasks to be done. At VTS that definition came from the board; in the SSH-US, that authorization came from the board, but only after the planning group shaped and defined the work to be done. Such groups found their work easier if they had access to some expertise—from inside the group and sometimes also from outside consultants. In Ocean City the church was blessed with a layman with planning and organizational skills from his secular job, and it had a pastor who had done graduate work in organizational development. The Lutheran congregation had a layman, Doug Germann, who helped define what format might help the members in their tasks. VTS called in a professional team (the Institute for Organizational Research and Development) the seminary had worked with previously.

These groups simply started where they were. A sense of need or opportunity arose somewhere, and it was tested and focused in a planning group. Not all of these planning groups started with official empowerment or authorization. If they did not have it in the beginning, they had to negotiate with their boards for that authorization. The process was not cut-and-dried; rather, it was dialogical from the beginning.

Early on, the planning group needs to determine what kind of process will be used. Consultants who have expertise and experience in more than one type of intervention are particularly helpful here. As the planning groups we studied were in dialogue with others, they worked on defining the theme, the purpose they wanted to further in the organization. They also established their calendar and organized themselves to do the work ahead. The dialogue engaged members as they listened to what visions others saw and identified the obstacles they needed to overcome. The task was to hear what vision or call was facing the congregation or organization and then to state that vision in as compelling a way as they could. That became the challenge and purpose for the large meeting. But by the time the planning group translated that vision into the theme of the big meeting, it was already a familiar concept to many in the organization. Talking about it brought many others on board. By then the planners had also discovered others—people in the community or other institutions, bishops or other denominational executives, pastors of neighboring churches, people from other seminaries—people "outside" their organization whose insights and ideas could be added to their own. Those people could bring valuable new perspectives that group members were unaware of.

All through the dialogue about vision, the planning group and the board—and, indeed, many ordinary members who had heard about and were excited by the conversation—recruited people whose insights were identified as being needed at the table. That broad recruiting process was essential. Every group that told us its story agreed that "getting all the people into the room" was critical.

## Stage Two: The Meeting

Each of the methods we have described here has its own protocols, but those may be modified to reflect the people who attend, the availability of communications technology (see how the Sacred Heart effort embraced a variety of technological methods to help communicate over distance), and planners' decisions about location, timing, and so forth.

We need to note here the creativity and flexibility of the processes. Almost each event included surprises—creative ways to form groups, shape questions, communicate findings from one group to the others, and use art and drama. Many of the groups noted that they also experienced the presence of God in what they were doing.

No more needs to be said about the meetings, because each is one of a kind. We have told you the stories of many places where planning groups, congregations, judicatories, and seminaries have engaged in just such efforts. None of these stories is exactly like any of the others, even when the same methods are used. These are not cookie-cutter events. The people who are there, their beliefs and commitments, the history of the group, the power of people working together to make things happen that they want to happen—all those will produce outcomes appropriate to that particular group at that particular time.

We have shared stories about four of the fifteen methods that have been identified for managing change. These methods have been sufficiently useful in enough different types of organizations that new methods are evolving from those we describe here.

# Stage 3: Ending and Beginning Again

It is in the period after the dramatic "big meeting" that the critical moments in long-term change occur. It is after the euphoria of a successful meeting that the real results begin to show up.

Many people who are attracted to these methods see the big meeting as the "pay dirt" of the approach. Our experience leads us to think of the big meeting as the catalyst for change, not the change itself. At best, the big meeting begins much more than it completes. It moves the life of the whole system, it brings new and unexpected ideas, it generates new energy, and it helps overcome differences and enables people to find common ground.

The time after the meeting is vital. The task then is to integrate the work of the meeting with the ordinary operations of the group. That is not what we are used to in planning efforts, however. Usually, the products of planning processes are assigned to standing committees or commissions of the organization. What we are clear about is that that approach usually does not work.

If the changes proposed are substantial, the new plan simply will not fit the pre-existing committees and organization. The structures and committees will need to be realigned to make it possible to follow the new path. The needed process is like the realignment we go through when we buy four new tires. Over the years of using the old tires, the wheels gradually "adjust" the old tires through wear and tear. Put on new tires, and very shortly they are worn in uneven ways, reflecting the alignment the car wheels had drifted into over months of wear. Similarly, the new patterns called for by a planning effort will wear badly on the old wheels—until the wheels are realigned and rebalanced to take the new into account.

To use another illustration, when a wagon driver decides to turn in a new direction, he is often unable to do so, because the ruts in the road are so deep that his mule cannot pull out of them. Until the driver and the mule together figure out how to get onto a new path, they will keep being drawn back into the ruts. Similarly, a pastor and congregation that have decided upon a new direction or two are often frustrated because the ruts of past experience and leadership keep pulling us back to the way things used to be. Clarity about a new direction will not be enough unless the processes and procedures of the organization itself are realigned toward the new direction.

In the Virginia Seminary case in chapter 5, after looking at the priorities the planning conference had set, the board acted to reshape each of its departmental budgets to fit the priorities set in the planning conference. The board spent months designing a new way to ensure that the newly chosen priorities were reflected in how the budget was made up, to make sure the planning affected management decisions. In Ocean City, St. Peter's United Methodist Church also made adjustments to budget processes, but in addition established new program activities to give flesh and blood to what the planners had dreamed at their conference.

In the Sacred Heart story it was the change process of this effort that both defined priorities for the future and pushed the priority-setting process back "upstairs," so that the order itself began setting priorities. Here, it was not the board that realigned the organization (as in the VTS case)—the change effort of the planning committee went "upstream" to the headquarters of the order itself. The planning activities gave a new way to focus on how the order did its work.

The most significant aspect of stage 3 is that unexpected things happen. We have come to expect it! Nobody at VTS went into the effort to change budget-making, but the new vision forced it to happen; nor did those in any of the other stories foresee quite what might come of their search for deeper visions.

The "big meeting" is a dramatic event that almost always opens up much new energy, puts new ideas on the table, and brings unheard perspectives into play. But it is just an event if the organization does not attempt to realign its operations and its committee work to be congruent with what was learned at the event.

Finally, we learned during our research, talking with dozens of people who have been through efforts like this, that the next step is to begin thinking two or three years down the pike to see what is ahead. Some groups in our stories started new groups for planning right away. Others developed clarity that "before long," perhaps two or five years or whenever the next big change occurred in the environment or the institution (transition of leadership, for example), it would be time for another event to broaden the vision for new opportunities.

In short, this whole process of engaging each other in envisioning the future put on the groups' agenda a continuing need to keep thinking about what lies ahead—for them as institutions, for the community in which they have a part, and for the many people who care about what they can become. The people who go through such explorations with each other begin to recognize that change is not "an event," even a dramatic event like that which they had just concluded. It is not something they have completed; it is something they have begun.

Change is a product of a rapidly changing environment, evolving religious and organizational needs, and growing knowledge about how leadership happens and organizations develop. So long as those realities are shifting and moving, the congregations and religious institutions will have to adapt continuously.

In our family of faith, we learned this truth from our patriarch and father Abraham. It was about four millennia ago that he looked up to the stars and heard a voice calling him to venture out from the familiar lands he knew in search of the future. Then and there the journey of faith began for him and for those who have followed him. It continues for us today. This book includes the stories of others who in a different time and place still try to follow that call and that vision. What we learn from them is that change is a process, not an event. It will never end for those who seek to follow a vision of the future.

# Epilogue
# A Note to Our Readers from Billie and Loren

OUR HOPE IN WRITING THIS BOOK IS THAT IT WILL BE HELPFUL TO our readers. Here are just a few reminders:

- You can't do it alone; you need the energy, wisdom, and commitment of the whole community.
- Build community; help the members of the congregation connect to each other.
- Give people the opportunity to have meaningful conversations with one another.
- It takes persistence. One meeting does not do it; you have to keep at it.
- After an event, work with others to maintain the culture that existed during the meeting and carry the change forward.

These are the logical and pragmatic things for leaders to keep in mind. Leaders might also have concerns or worries ("fear" is probably too strong a word). Do we really want to rock the boat? Isn't there value in keeping things stable, safe, without risk? Who knows where the use of some of these methods might lead?

Here are some questions that a pastor friend of ours who uses these methods has asked himself:

- Am I open to a process in which I do not determine the outcomes?

- Am I willing to enter into a shared visioning process in order to discern the congregation's long-term vision?
- Am I willing to invest energy to change the congregation's orbit and work toward transforming the culture?

Years ago, Loren was a young Episcopal priest running a very complex conference. He knew how to run it, and he was good at it. But a moment came three-quarters of the way through when all of a sudden he ran out of gas or ideas or agenda. He just didn't have a clue what to do next. Thirty people were sitting there, waiting for the next shoe to drop. He was up front, standing there with his mouth open, running on empty. He paused and sat down. He felt he had failed. Suddenly a woman made a comment that fit right in. And then one of the men responded to her, and others joined in. It all came together in ways Loren didn't understand and couldn't ever replicate. Loren says, "What happened was that when I got out of the way, things happened. I had no answers, but the people in the room had the answers." This is what the first two bullet points above are about.

Billie had a similar experience. She was working with a city where 250 citizens had gathered in a Future Search conference to do something about this city, where violence was on the increase. The citizens wanted to work on transforming the city into a city "free from fear." People at the meeting were from every walk of life: businesspeople, clergy, police, high-school students, teachers, politicians, and physicians. As the conference progressed, Billie remembers worrying, "Will it all come together?" Then a woman came up, put her arm around Billie, and whispered, "It's going great! Look around you, and feel the energy. The *Spirit* is working here. Trust that!"

# Appendix A
# Checklists

## Checklist 1: Focus on Congregations

Take a few minutes to review this list of challenges and hold it up against the life of the group of which you are a leader. Make a check in the space provided to the left if in your opinion the challenge is one you are facing at this moment.

___ 1. Many of our members seem unclear about what we are all about, what we stand for, what our mission is.

___ 2. Our educational programs are not designed for adults who want to engage in serious learning about being disciples.

___ 3. Some of our members think the congregation needs a vision for the future.

___ 4. In the past few years, we have been losing more members than we are gaining, and we are unclear about how to attract new members.

___ 5. Demographic changes have occurred in our neighborhood.

___ 6. We have an aging congregation, and many of our biggest donors are in their sixties and seventies.

___ 7. In our congregation we don't seem to be "connected" to one another as we used to be.

___ 8. We do not feel very connected to our regional and national offices.

___ 9. Money is a big worry, and we regularly defer maintenance on our building and grounds, as well as short-
change administrative support.

___ 10. To tell the truth, we don't relate much to other congregations of our own denomination—much less to
others.

___ 11. We have a hard time recruiting, motivating, and training new leaders for our key committees.

___ 12. We do not talk about controversial issues, even important ones.

___ 13. Our outreach and mission work is not as strong as it
used to be.

___ 14. Our worship life needs to be enriched. We keep hearing "same old, same old" about worship.

___ 15. We need to attract younger people and families.

___ 16. We are not keeping abreast of new technologies that
might enhance our worship services, administration,
and outreach.

___ 17. We have difficulty accepting change.

If you have checked even one of these 17 items, you have
identified a challenge that the rest of this book will help you
explore and address.

Next, go down the left margin (right next to your check
marks), and indicate with an asterisk all the issues you consider
seriously troubling. If you like, put two, three, or even four
asterisks to indicate the intensity of your concern.

# Checklist 2: Focus on Religious Institutions

The following list of issues is for people who serve in theological seminaries, judicatory offices, and other religious non-parochial organizations. If that's where you spend most of your time, these questions may help you discover areas in which you may need to consider change.

Make a check in the space provided to the left if you think this issue is a real concern for your institution.

__ 1. Membership losses worry us. Membership is slipping, and contributions that sustain our work are diminishing.

__ 2. Population changes complicate our life. We need to be active and visible in areas where we are not; and we need to pick up our tents and pull out of some areas where we are currently working.

__ 3. The sense of connection has eroded within the organization, among people in the various geographic areas we serve, and between the organization and those whom we serve.

__ 4. Money is a worry.

__ 5. Our relations with other regions and our national office are not very useful or satisfying.

__ 6. We operate as if we were in separate silos, with very little sense of the whole. People work in their departments on their piece of the action, at times unrelated to what others are doing or to the overall vision. Horizontal communication is poor.

__ 7. We do not know whether we are serving the needs of our constituents.

__ 8. Volunteers are hard to recruit and even harder to motivate.

\_\_ 9.  Professional development, if it happens at all, is self-directed, with no consideration of the leadership needs of the whole.

\_\_ 10.  We often spend inordinate amounts of time on parts of the system that are not functioning well, neglecting the healthier parts.

\_\_ 11.  We need to develop programs and educational systems that will help both clergy and laity in our changing world.

\_\_ 12.  We don't keep up with or use technology well.

\_\_ 13.  People in our organization are polarized about change, some championing the need for change while others want to keep things as they are.

If you have checked even one of these issues as a current concern of your organization, you may find it helpful to check your impressions with those of others—your board, faculty or key division leaders, or staff people.

Next, go down the left margin (right next to your check marks), and indicate with an asterisk all the issues you consider seriously troubling. If you like, put two, three, or even four asterisks to indicate the intensity of your concern.

# Appendix B
# Frequently Asked Questions

1. *How do these participative methods affect the role and authority of the pastor/rabbi or board members?*

We believe they strengthen these roles. They generate acknowledgement and ownership of the challenges that need to be addressed. They develop commitment to the values, mission, and vision that have been jointly established. Horizontal and vertical communications are reinforced through discussion and deliberation. People feel they are a part of the whole, true members.

2. *Do we need an outside consultant?*

We would suggest it. A neutral person with expertise in large-group methods can be very helpful. If you have someone in the congregation who does this type of work, you might team that person up with an outside consultant.

3. *How large is large?*

This is a question frequently asked by small congregations. If the number of external and internal stakeholders is over thirty, face-to-face conversation will be more difficult, and airtime for people to voice their views will not be in great supply. Introverts often find it more difficult to speak up in a larger group. With a group larger than thirty, these methods would assist you.

4. *How can a consultant run a meeting like this if he or she doesn't understand our faith and culture?*

The consultant works with a planning team that can provide the consultant with an understanding of the background and culture of the congregation or institution. The planning team can also include in the conference design some moments for worship, prayer, reflection, and singing. A number of congregations and judicatories have ended a large-group gathering with a worship service in celebration of what has been accomplished together.

5. *How do we get everyone in the congregation to come?*

Congregational leadership plays an important role in emphasizing the importance of the conference. There is no doubt that posters, letters, notices in bulletins, and encouragement by the clergy are all good, but person-to-person recruiting, often done by the planning committee and the board members, is the most effective outreach tool. Invitations should strongly stress how much the invitee's thoughts and ideas are welcomed and needed.

6. *Who is included in a Future Search or an Appreciative Inquiry Summit?*

The recruitment phase is very important. The planning team and the board should be involved in identifying key stakeholders to ensure broad representation at the meeting. The objective is to create a microcosm of the whole organization. This would naturally include representation from all the various groups: youth, faith educators, facility managers, finance committee members, staff, pastors, mission groups, members of the community within which the congregation operates, and others. Even if some people cannot attend, make sure you have a group that is representative of the congregation. These methods develop ownership, increase volunteerism, help bring new leaders to the surface, and energize longtime leaders.

### 7. *What about outside stakeholders?*

We think a few outside stakeholders add value. You might include someone from the denomination's regional or national office. It could be a representative from agencies in the community with which the outreach group works or a local pastor or rabbi with whom the congregation has worked. Much depends on the purpose of the conference. The question to ask is, "Who are the people outside our membership who have a stake in this organization, community, or institution?"

### 8. *How much time do these methods really require?*

Future Search and the Appreciative Inquiry Summit usually take two days, beginning and ending with a half-day and working a full day in between. For example, starting Thursday evening, then continuing all day Friday, and closing early afternoon on Saturday would total two days. This is an important topic for the planning committee to discuss. If these gatherings that involve all the stakeholders around issues that matter are worth doing, then they are worth doing well. Spending the necessary time for discussion and reflection is important. There is power in having two nights to sleep, dream, and think over the preceding days' events. It is also important to stress that unlike other meetings, these are not drop-in events. People who come must commit to staying the whole time. Complex larger systems like a judicatory, seminary, or other religious institution may need more time for implementing changes, and these activities may go on for several years. (See examples in chapter 5.)

9. *How do these methods deal with differences of opinion? Is there a potential of turning a meeting like this into a free-for-all?*

These methods are designed to bring people together to discover areas upon which they can agree. The methods include guidelines for holding worthy conversations; people speak freely about what they believe without denigrating the views of others. Some of the time is spent in mixed groups where participants can listen to a variety of perspectives on issues. These conversations are often eye-opening for the participants as they hear and understand different views, even if they do not always agree with them. People enjoy being in an environment where they can connect with others, have meaningful conversations, build new relationships, and feel that their thoughts and ideas are valued. Differences of opinion that can't be quickly resolved are noted, but the majority of the time is spent on areas of agreement. The search for common ground is continually stressed.

10. *How does the process work when there are existing committees, boards, and leaders?*

These methods do not set aside existing roles or committees. Existing committees may take on some new initiatives. New committees may be formed for a special purpose. Leaders may emerge who want to work with others on a special need or a particular project. In some cases the board may set up special committees or assign certain responsibilities to existing committees. We believe, however, that if the gathering proposes a new direction, it is important to explore the degree to which the current structures, committees, and communication methods can support the new direction. This question needs to be asked.

11. *Will these methods help us move from planning to action?*

These methods do not stop with the planning; they go on to action. Supports are built in, and follow-up activities take place to make sure that the desired outcomes are occurring. Several congregations have appointed a task force to shepherd the vision and report regularly to the congregation on actions being taken and initiatives being implemented.

12. *How often should one of these "whole system in the room" meetings occur?*

Large-group gatherings should be held whenever there are issues that need to involve the whole system, perhaps every two or three years. Continual scanning of both the external and internal environment can help determine when an event is needed. "How are we doing?" is an important question to ask periodically. Two of the examples in the book are about congregations going through a transition after a pastor of many years leaves or retires.

13. *When would you use Open Space and World Café?*

Open Space and World Café, since they can be done in a shorter period of time, are a good way to identify people's concerns. These methods are also a great way to build community. They help people connect with those who have similar ideas and interests. World Café is a unique way to help people explore an important issue. It could easily be done at an extended coffee hour or as an evening program. Open Space is often used as the action-planning phase of a Future Search or an Appreciative Inquiry Summit. After new initiatives have been posted, people are asked to sign up for the initiative they want to sponsor, take on, or be part of. They then come together and plan actions and time frames and identify the support and help they may need.

14. *What happens when there is a turnover in the leadership, particularly the rabbi or pastor?*

This is a very important question. Two of the stories in chapter 4 reflect a change occurring around a pastor/rabbi transition. In searching for a new leader, not only is a profile important, but in the interview candidates should be asked the questions that the congregation, after using a Future Search–type process, agrees are important areas to explore with potential new leaders. Make sure the congregational or institutional initiatives are going to be nurtured and maintained. We suggest that you ask those being interviewed if they are familiar with these participative processes.

15. *How long will it take to plan a Future Search or an Appreciative Inquiry Summit?*

Several weeks or even months of planning and preparation are needed. The board appoints a planning team from the congregation; the pastor/rabbi and one or two board members should be members. This team, with the consultant, will decide the dates and the details. A very important task of the team is to establish the purpose and invite the members, friends, and stakeholders.

## 16. *Is it necessary to use an off-site facility?*

We don't think it is necessary to move off-site if a large room on-site will accommodate all the participants. The cost of travel and the expense of an off-site facility may make the use of the worship center or a nearby meeting space desirable. Seemingly minor logistical issues are actually very important. Ample, convenient parking is key.

# Appendix C
# Suggested Resources

## How-to Books on Large Group Methods

The following books are excellent sources for learning about the individual methods and how to use them.

Axelrod, Richard, and Emily Axelrod. *The Conference Model: Collaborating for Change.* San Francisco: Barrett-Koehler, 2000. This method was not described in this book, but it is a combination of Future Search and a process for aligning the organizational structure to the desired future. We do not know whether any faith-based institution has used this approach. It could easily be modified for this purpose.

Brown, Juanita, and David Isaacs. *The World Café: Shaping Our Futures through Conversations That Matter.* San Francisco: Barrett-Koehler, 2005.

Dannemiller Tyson Associates. *Whole Scale Change: Unleashing the Magic in Organizations.* San Francisco: Barrett-Koehler, 2000.

Ludema, James D., Diana Whitney, Bernard J. Mohr, and Thomas J. Griffin. *The Appreciative Inquiry Summit: A Practitioner's Guide for Leading Large Group Change.* San Francisco: Barrett-Koehler, 2003.

Weisbord, Marvin, and Sandra Janoff. *Future Search: An Action Guide to Finding Common Ground in Organizations and Communities,* 2nd ed. San Francisco: Barrett-Koehler, 2002.

# Other Books and Articles on Large Group Methods

The books and journal publications that follow, in addition to giving an overview of these methods, describe how they have been applied in both the public and private sectors.

Alban, Billie T., and Barbara Benedict Bunker, eds. Special Issue on Large Group Interventions, *Journal of Applied Behavioral Science* 28, no. 4 (December 1, 1992). Thousand Oaks, Calif.: Sage Publications, 1992.

————. Special Issue on Large Group Interventions, *Journal of Applied Behavioral Science* 41, no. 1 (March 1, 2005). Thousand Oaks, Calif.: Sage Publications, 2005.

Bunker, Barbara Benedict, and Billie T. Alban. *The Handbook of Large Group Methods: Creating Systemic Change in Organizations and Communities.* San Francisco: Jossey-Bass, 2006.

————. *Large Group Interventions: Engaging the Whole System for Rapid Change.* San Francisco: Jossey-Bass, 1997.

Holman, Peggy, and Tom Devane. *The Change Handbook: Group Methods for Shaping the Future.* San Francisco: Barrett-Koehler, 1999.

# Congregational Studies

These two books made "Congregational Studies" a discipline in many seminaries and graduate schools. Both explore varied perspectives on what congregations are and how they work. Anyone working with congregational change needs to be acquainted with them. Chapters from *Handbook of Congre-*

*gational Studies,* which is out of print, can be downloaded for free at *http://hirr.hartsem.edu.*

Ammerman, Nancy Tatom, Jackson W. Carroll, Carl S. Dudley, and William McKinney. *Studying Congregations: A New Handbook.* Nashville: Abingdon, 1998.
Carroll, Jackson W., Carl S. Dudley, and William McKinney. *Handbook of Congregational Studies.* Nashville: Abingdon Press, 1986.

# Churches Look to the Future

These four small books provide a framework for the historical and current dynamics that make changing congregations both essential and difficult.

Mead, Loren. *Financial Meltdown in the Mainline.* Bethesda: Alban Institute, 1998. Mead opens up many of the financial difficulties facing congregations and other religious institutions.
———. *Five Challenges for the Once and Future Church.* Bethesda: Alban Institute, 1996.
———. *The Once and Future Church.* Washington: Alban Institute, 1991; Bethesda: Alban Institute, 1994.
———. *Transforming Congregations for the Future.* Bethesda: Alban Institute, 1994.

## Changing Congregations

Several other books are particularly useful in thinking about changing congregations.

Bass, Diana Butler. *The Practicing Congregation.* Herndon, Va.: Alban Institute, 2004.

———. *Christianity for the Rest of Us*. San Francisco: Harper, 2006.

Bass, Richard, ed. *Leadership in Congregations*. Herndon, Va.: Alban Institute, 2006.

Oswald, Roy M., and Claire S. Burkat. *Transforming Regional Bodies*. Boonsboro, Md.: Life Structure Resources, 2001.

Rendle, Gilbert R. *Leading Change in Congregations*. Bethesda: Alban Institute, 1998.

Robinson, Anthony B. *Transforming Congregational Culture*. Grand Rapids: Eerdmans, 2003.

Sellon, Mary K., Daniel P. Smith, and Gail F. Grossman. *Redeveloping the Congregation: A How-To for Lasting Change*. Herndon, Va.: Alban Institute, 2002.

Steinke, Peter L. *Congregational Leadership in Anxious Times*. Herndon, Va.: Alban Institute, 2006.

Thumma, Scott, and Dave Travis. *Beyond Megachurch Myths: What We Can Learn from America's Largest Churches*. San Francisco: Jossey-Bass, 2007. This last book is a must-read for mainline institutions. Rather than groan about megachurches, the book describes what we can learn from them.

## Web Sites

www.futuresearch.net
www.openspaceworld.org
www.appreciativeinquiry.case.edu
www.theworldcafe.com
www.resourcingchristianity.org